bowl food

bowl food

over 75 recipes for satisfying smoothie bowls,
salads, soups, noodles, stews and more

rps

RYLAND PETERS & SMALL
LONDON • NEW YORK

Senior designer Toni Kay
Commissioning editor Stephanie Milner
Picture manager Christina Borsi
Editorial assistant Ella Bukbardis
Head of Production Patricia Harrington
Art director Leslie Harrington
Editorial director Julia Charles
Publisher Cindy Richards
Indexer Vanessa Bird

First published in 2017 by
Ryland Peters & Small
20–21 Jockey's Fields, London WC1R 4BW
and
341 E 116th St, New York NY 10029
www.rylandpeters.com

10 9 8 7 6 5 4 3 2 1

Recipe collection compiled by Stephanie Milner

Text copyright © Bronte Aurell, Miranda Ballard, Ghillie Basan, Jordan Bourke, Ross Dobson, Mat Follas, Amy Ruth Finegold, Nicola Graimes, Dunja Gulin, Vicky Jones, Uyen Luu, Louise Pickford, Shelagh Ryan, Janet Sawyer, Sarah Wilkinson, Jenna Zoe and Ryland Peters & Small 2017

Design and photographs copyright © Ryland Peters & Small 2017

ISBN: 978-1-84975-821-5

Printed in China

A CIP record for this book is available from the British Library.

US Library of Congress Cataloging-in-Publication Data has been applied for.

Notes:
• Both British (Metric) and American (Imperial plus US cups) measurements are included in these recipes for your convenience, however it is important to work with one set of measurements and not alternate between the two within a recipe.
• All spoon measurements are level unless otherwise specified.
• All eggs are medium (UK) or large (US), unless specified as large, in which case US extra-large should be used. Uncooked or partially cooked eggs should not be served to the very old, frail, young children, pregnant women or those with compromised immune systems.
• Ovens should be preheated to the specified temperatures. We recommend using an oven thermometer. If using a fan-assisted oven, adjust temperatures according to the manufacturer's instructions.
• When a recipe calls for the grated zest of citrus fruit, buy unwaxed fruit and wash well before using. If you can only find treated fruit, scrub well in warm soapy water before using.
• To sterilize preserving jars, wash them in hot, soapy water and rinse in boiling water. Place in a large saucepan and cover with hot water. With the saucepan lid on, bring the water to a boil and continue boiling for 15 minutes. Turn off the heat and leave the jars in the hot water until just before they are to be filled. Invert the jars onto a clean kitchen cloth to dry. Sterilize the lids for 5 minutes, by boiling or according to the manufacturer's instructions. Jars should be filled and sealed while they are still hot.

Contents

Introduction 6

Build your Bowl 8

FABULOUS FRUITS 10

PUNCHY PULSES, GRAINS AND SEEDS 28

VIBRANT VEGETABLES 60

MIGHTY MEAT AND POULTRY 90

FRESH FISH AND SEAFOOD 118

Index 142

Credits 144

Introduction

The phrase 'bowl food' has become synonymous with wholesome comfort eating. Enjoying food eaten out of a generous serving bowl with a fork, spoon (or chopsticks) is a modern indulgence to cherish. And what makes up the bowl extends far beyond just soups! Whether it's a breakfast bowl, a salad or a slow-cooked stews – what brings all styles of bowl food together is their nourishing balance of vegetables, fruit, whole grains and a good source of protein, whether it is animal or plant-based. Noodles, rice, pulses and grains are all an excellent base for any bowl, providing a starting point for whichever vegetables, meat or fish you decide to pair it with. With the days of structured meal times becoming rarer, and a rise in the popularity of superfoods and high-protein diets, bowl food can be enjoyed on a daily basis to ensure you're well nourished, energized and satisfied.

In terms of nutrients, if a whole grain is the base of your bowl (see the Pink Quinoa Salad with Fennel & Arame on page 47), this will mean the inclusion of several B vitamins such as thiamine and riboflavin, which are thought to play a role in speeding up our metabolisms. A sweeter option would be the Honey & Vanilla Granola Bowl (see page 31), homemade granola being an impressive source of fibre/fiber and iron. If a lighter bowl is needed, look no further than the Sesame-coated Tofu with Adzuki Beans (see page 51). The high protein content here will help you stay fuller for longer. Fast and fresh salads pop up frequently in this book, as preparing one is a quick yet eating it still a satisfying experience. What makes a truly delicious salad (such as the Spiralized Summer Salad with Smoked Mackerel on page 71), is a good selection of fresh vegetables, a tasty source of protein and a punchy dressing to bring all the flavours and textures together.

The book begins with Build Your Bowl – a basic introduction to how to set about constructing your own perfect bowl of food. You'll find suggestions for different bases, proteins and dressings that you can mix and match to create your own new favourites. The recipes themselves are then split into chapters organized by the key food groups, starting with Fabulous Fruits (where you'll find a delicious Chia Seed Breakfast Bowl on page 19), then comes Punchy Pulses, Grains & Seeds (try the Hemp Tabbouleh with Pea and Mint Falafel on page 48). Next Vibrant Vegetables, features a stunning recipe for a Smoked Aubergine/Eggplant & Red Pepper Salad (see page 88) and of course Asian-style food is particularly well suited to a bowl-serve. In Mighty Meat & Poultry you'll find plenty such options to enjoy, including the popular Korean dish Bibimbap (see page 109) and in Fresh Fish & Seafood Shrimp Pad Thai on page 133. All of the delicious and creative recipes included here will inspire you to build your own balanced and beautiful bowls to be enjoyed at any time of the day, all year round.

Build your Bowl

The base of your bowl should be a protein-rich foundation for your meal. This can be any of your favourite grains, such as the more commonly used brown rice, which is used in the delicious Egyptian dish Koshari (see page 56), lentils, or seeds such as quinoa or spelt, as presented in the Artichoke Salad with Spelt Grains (see page 39). Where noodles are concerned, using soba noodles, or if the sweet potato kind appeal to you, the Sweet Potato Noodles with Broccoli in Black Bean Sauce (see page 76) are great if you want something different. For a sweet and filling breakfast bowls, using traditional oats, or more unusually, using rye bread to create your porridge results in a hearty Danish breakfast, as shown in Rye Bread Porridge with Skyr and Toasted Hazelnuts (see page 16).

ADDING FRUIT AND VEGETABLES

The layering of fruit and vegetables, both cooked and uncooked, are perfect to create satisfyingly textured bowl. Solely fruit can make up the smoothie bowls in Fresh and Fruity, the beautiful Mexican Horchata Smoothie (see page 15) is simply stunning in both taste and colour. The Hemp Tabbouleh with Pea and Mint Falafel (see page 48) is a perfect example of how some simply chopped up vegetables and herbs can bulk up a bowl. For a crunchy bright bowl, a combination of salad on any chosen base, or even to be used as the base is the perfect quick meal. Don't be afraid to try making your own pickles, such as the kimchi in the Kimchi, Avocado and Alfalfa Salad (see page 75), if you are feeling brown rice may be too heavy, this is the perfect contrast.

PROTEIN POWER

Protein plays a large part in these bowls, with no bowl being complete without ingredients such as quinoa, fish, chicken or tofu. Excellent examples of protein-rich bowls would be the Moroccan Chicken Tagine with Brown Lentils (see page 114) or Korean-style Mapo Tofu (see page 93). For most, if not all, the savoury recipes an extra boost of protein could definitely be added by soft boiled or poached egg. Other veggie protein options could be halloumi, tempeh or pulses whizzed into hummus. The chia seeds in the Chia Seed Breakfast Bowl (see page 19) are the perfect protein breakfast fix. Another idea would be to add a spoonful of peanut butter to porridge for another slow-burning boost.

THE EXTRAS

No bowl is complete without a topping, sauce, or dressing to add the final element to a great bowl of food. Smoothie bowl toppings are vital to bring the bowl together, these can range from sliced fruits and berries to chia seeds and chopped nuts. A sauce like the pesto in the Spaghetti Squash with Tofu, Nori and Kale Pesto (see page 55) or the salsa for the Cuban Black Bean and Red Pepper Soup (see page 36) really bring the bowls flavours together in a perfect flavourful harmony.

FABULOUS FRUITS

Matcha is the finely ground powder of a particular variety of green tea grown uniquely in Japan. It has great health benefits as the whole leaf is ground giving higher amounts of antioxidants than other teas. Also high in fibre and chlorophyll, matcha is not only nutritious but adds an alluring sweet nutty flavour to smoothies – it is also a fabulous green colour!

Matcha tea, banana and sesame smoothie bowl

2 large bananas
2 teaspoons matcha tea
250 ml/generous1 cup coconut
   milk, plus extra to serve
300 ml/1 1/3 cups sheep's milk
   yogurt
2 tablespoons tahini paste
50 g/1 scant cup baby spinach
   leaves
2 tablespoons honey

Toppings

20 g/1/4 cup sliced banana
toasted sesame seeds
red fruits, such as raspberries
   and pomegranate seeds

Serves 2

Peel and roughly chop 1 1/2 bananas and put in a blender with the matcha tea, coconut milk, yogurt, tahini paste, spinach leaves and honey. Blend until really smooth. Divide between two bowls.

Thinly slice the remaining banana and arrange on top of the bowls with the sesame seeds and fruit. Drizzle over a little extra coconut milk and serve.

Tip: You can decorate your smoothie with any type of fruit although the red fruits are a particularly attractive contrast and add even more antioxidants.

This is based on the Mexican almond or rice milk beverage mixed with cinnamon: horchata. Here it is blended with exotic fruits, nuts and chia seeds. You can really please yourself as to what fruit you include, depending on both preference and availability.

Mexican horchata smoothie

1 small mango (250 g/9 oz. or 125 g/4½ oz. peeled and stoned/pitted weight), roughly diced

½ small pineapple (250 g/9 oz. or 125 g/4½ oz. peeled and cored weight), roughly diced

1 small banana, peeled and chopped

250 g/9 oz. exotic fruits, such as dragon fruit, guava, passionfruit and so on

250 ml/1 cup almond or rice milk

1 teaspoon ground cinnamon

freshly squeezed juice 1 lime

2 tablespoons roughly chopped brazil nuts

1 tablespoon agave syrup, plus extra to drizzle

40 g/¼ cup chia seeds

Topping

sliced fruits
chia seeds
passionfruit
toasted coconut
shavings

Serves 2

Put all the fruit, rice milk, ground cinnamon, lime juice, brazil nuts, agave syrup and chia seeds in a blender and purée until really smooth. Divide between two bowls.

Arrange the sliced fruits and coconut over the smoothie, sprinkle with chia seeds and drizzle over a little extra agave syrup, if desired.

There is no better way to start the day than with a big steaming bowl of porridge. Store-bought mixes are full of sugar and added nasties, so try making your own with this recipe, which uses a base of both oats and rye flakes. It takes a little longer to cook, but the result is a wholesome and tasty bowlful.

Oat and rye porridge with lingonberries

80 g/1 cup minus
   1 tablespoon old-
   fashioned rolled oats
20 g/1 tablespoon rye
   flakes
225 ml/1 cup minus
1 tablespoon whole milk
a pinch of salt
small knob/pat of butter
   (optional)
pumpkin and sunflower
   seeds, to serve

Stirred lingonberries

250 g/9 oz. frozen
   lingonberries (available
   in some speciality food
   stores and online)
100 g/½ cup caster/
   granulated sugar

Serves 2

In a saucepan, boil the oats and rye in the milk and 225 ml/1 cup of cold water, reserving 1 tablespoon of each to use later if needed. Simmer while continuously stirring for 5–7 minutes or until the oats and rye are cooked. Add a pinch of salt to taste and a little of the reserved water and/or milk if a looser texture is required. For extra creaminess, you can add a small knob/pat of butter and stir through.

To prepare the stirred lingonberries simply add the caster/granulated sugar and stir. Leave for a while and then stir again, until the sugar dissolves and the berries have defrosted. Store any leftover stirred lingonberries in the fridge. You can add a pinch of cinnamon or a drop of vanilla extract to the stirred lingonberries, if liked.

Spoon the hot porridge into serving bowls, add a good dollop of stirred lingonberries and top with pumpkin seeds and sunflower seeds. Serve while still warm.

The shiny chia seeds have recently been rediscovered and are referred to as 'an ancient American superfood'. Rich in calcium and omega-3 and -6 fatty acids, they are nutritionally very similar to flax and sesame seeds, and should therefore become part of everybody's diet. This quick breakfast bowl, topped with fresh fruit and nuts will fill your tummy for many hours!

Chia seed breakfast bowl

40 g/¼ cup chia seeds
2 tablespoons (dark) raisins or
  other dried fruits
230 ml/1 scant cup nut milk
a pinch of sea salt
⅛ teaspoon bourbon vanilla
  powder or ground cinnamon
2 tablespoons raw or dry-roasted
  mixed nuts
fresh fruit, chopped (optional)

Serves 1

In a bowl, mix the chia seeds and dried fruits. Lightly warm the nut milk in a small saucepan, add the salt and vanilla or cinnamon, and pour it over the seeds and leave it to soak for 10 minutes.

If you only have raw nuts, preheat the oven to 180°C (350°F) Gas 4, spread the nuts on a tray and roast for 10–14 minutes, stirring occasionally. When the nuts start cracking and releasing their oils, that's when they're done. Be careful not to burn them, as this can happen easily, so it's best to check how they're doing after 8–10 minutes and continue roasting for a couple more minutes if they're not done. Transfer them onto a plate and wait for them to cool slightly. Chop them coarsely and sprinkle over the porridge, along with a little chopped fresh fruit, if desired.

Dry-roasted nuts are great as a healthy snack and as an addition to cakes, cookies, salads — to anything really!

Having an açaí bowl literally feels like eating ice cream for breakfast, and there are loads of fun ways to make them. If you are making these bowls for children, set up a toppings station and let them pick their own; it's a great way to start getting them more connected with what's going into their bodies. Açaí is one of the only fruits that contains omega-3 fatty acids, it has double the antioxidants of blueberries and is fantastically energizing. All you have to do is a blend the base until smooth, then top with whatever you like. Look for puréed açaí packs in the frozen section of your grocery store, or else you can also go for the powdered version.

Açaí bowls galore

1 pack frozen açaí purée
   (about 100 ml/⅓ cup)
1 frozen banana (see Note)
200 ml/¾ cup almond milk

To serve

20 g/¼ cup desiccated/
   shredded coconut
goji berries
strawberries, sliced banana
   or kiwi (optional)

Serves 2

Put the açaí purée, frozen banana and almond milk in a food processor and blend together until smooth.

Pour the mixture into bowls and sprinkle with desiccated/shredded coconut and goji berries. Serve with fruit – a variety will work well here; try strawberries, banana or kiwi slices.

Note: To freeze the banana, peel as many as you would like and put in a freezer bag in the freezer for at least 8 hours or overnight. You can freeze the bananas well in advance as they will keep frozen for up to 2 weeks.

Variations: There are many ways to make this bowlful of goodness. Substitute the açaí purée for 5 frozen strawberries and top with extra strawberries and cacao nibs, or use 30 g/¼ cup frozen blueberries instead of the açaí purée and top with sliced kiwi and coconut chips. For an extra thick fruit base, add an extra frozen banana, or try blending in 2 teaspoons of cacao powder, then top with almond butter and hemp seeds for a chocolate and nut variation. Other fun toppings include a handful of grain-free granola, a dollop of plain/natural or coconut yogurt, crushed seeds and nuts, or any sliced fruit you desire.

Good fats help balance the body's blood sugar levels to maintain a healthy weight. Paired with the omega-3-rich berry chia compote, this is true beauty food!

Coconut yogurt with berry chia swirl

2 x 400-ml/14-oz. cans full-fat coconut milk
2 probiotic supplement capsules (such as Acidophilus or a broad-spectrum probiotic)
1 heaped teaspoon stevia, to sweeten
1 teaspoon lemon juice
60g/½ cup pistachio nuts, roughly chopped

Berry chia compote

140 g/1 cup strawberries, chopped
120 g/1 cup raspberries, chopped
2 teaspoons freshly squeezed lemon juice
3 tablespoons ground chia seeds
2 teaspoons stevia

a 400-g/14-oz. capacity sterilized glass jar with an airtight lid

Serves 2–4

Put the cans of coconut milk in the fridge for at least 8 hours, or overnight; this will solidify the healthy coconut fats and separate them from the liquid.

Once chilled, open the cans and carefully scoop off the 'cream' that has risen to the top, discarding the liquid at the bottom. Put the coconut cream in a food processor with the contents of the probiotic supplement capsules, stevia and lemon juice. Blend until well combined, then spoon the mixture into the sterilized glass jar. Carefully tap the jar on the counter to get rid of any air pockets. Wipe the jar clean and screw on the lid.

Set the sealed mixture in the oven with the light on but without actually turning the heat on for 24 hours – this ensures a warm, constant temperature that will encourage fermentation. Next, refrigerate it for 3 hours – this is when it will start to thicken.

To make the berry chia jam/jelly, put the strawberries, raspberries and lemon juice in a saucepan or pot set over medium heat. Warm through, and when the berries start to soften mash them roughly by hand using a fork or potato masher. Add the ground chia seeds and stir to combine; the mixture will thicken a little. Remove the pan from the heat, add the stevia and stir until dissolved. Cover and chill in the fridge for at least 30 minutes to allow the mixture to set. The jam/jelly can be eaten straight away or stored in a sterilized glass jar or airtight container in the fridge for up to 3–5 days.

Once the yogurt is chilled, serve in small bowls with 2 tablespoons of jam/jelly stirred through and pistachio nuts sprinkled on top. It also goes well served with granola or sliced fresh fruit. The yogurt will keep for up to 2 weeks if stored in an airtight container in the fridge.

This porridge, known as 'Øllebrød' in Danish, features in the Academy-Award-winning Danish movie *Babette's Feast*. It is a very old recipe for rye-bread porridge and was originally a way to use leftover rye bread and drabs of beer, hence the name *Øllebrød*, which translates as 'bread and beer soup'. You can make it with a malt beer or ale, but it's just as nice made with water. Some people eat *Øllebrød* as a dessert, but it also makes the perfect hearty breakfast.

Rye-bread porridge with skyr and toasted hazelnuts

200 g/7 oz. dark rye bread (ideally not seeded)
1 strip of unwaxed orange peel (2.5-cm/1-inch diameter)
½ teaspoon ground cinnamon
¼ teaspoon cocoa powder
40 g/3 tablespoons caster/granulated sugar
1–2 teaspoons freshly squeezed orange juice
skyr or plain/natural yogurt, toasted hazelnuts (roughly chopped) and fresh berries, to serve

Serves 2–3

Cut the rye bread into small pieces, then add to a saucepan. Cover with 600 ml/2⅓ cups of water. Leave to soak for at least 15 minutes (or overnight in the fridge).

Add the orange peel, cinnamon and cocoa and bring to the boil. Leave to simmer for around 15–20 minutes until all bread has dissolved and you are left with what looks like a very thick gravy. Remove the orange peel. Add the sugar (hold back a little bit in case you prefer a less sweet version). Add the orange juice (you can add a little more, to taste). There may be the odd lump of bread left – I quite like these, but you can push it through a sieve/ strainer if you prefer a smoother version.

If you have used seeded rye bread, the seeds will still be present. You can pulse the mixture a few times in a food processor if you want a smoother consistency.

Serve hot with a dollop of skyr (or plain yogurt), toasted hazelnuts and fresh berries, such as blueberries or raspberries. If serving as a dessert, add double/heavy cream instead of yogurt.

The typical diet in Western countries today contains far fewer omega-3 fatty acids than the human diet of a century ago, and it's not a good thing. We should try to include as many foods rich in omega-3s as we can (such as flaxseed and chia seeds, walnuts, soybeans and tofu) because they are essential for a healthy, working metabolism.

Omega-3-rich breakfast bowl

6 tablespoons flaxseed, ground into flour (see method)
480 ml/2 cups plain/natural yogurt
4 tablespoons chia seeds
200 g/2 very ripe bananas, peeled
fresh lemon balm leaves, to garnish

a sterilized glass jar with an airtight lid (optional)

Serves 2

To make flaxseed flour, grind the flaxseed in a high-speed blender or spice grinder into a fine flour. Do this just before consuming it, or grind it in advance and keep in a sealed jar in the fridge until you're ready to use it (it will keep for 1 week in the fridge). Do not buy pre-ground flaxseed because it loses most of its nutrients a few days after grinding and becomes rancid very quickly.

In a big bowl mix the yogurt with the flaxseed flour and chia seeds and let sit for 10 minutes, allowing the chia seeds to soften. Chop the bananas, fold in and serve. Decorate with fresh lemon balm for a refreshing green colour and a nice lemony aroma.

PUNCHY PULSES, GRAINS AND SEEDS

Granola is the ultimate well-being breakfast. It has become very fashionable, and you can, of course, vary the ingredients to include your favourites. This recipe calls for a combination of honey and vanilla to flavour the grains and seeds, spruced up with a mixture of dried fruits.

Honey and vanilla granola bowl

250 g/1 cup clear honey, plus extra to drizzle
1 teaspoon vanilla paste, or seeds from 1 vanilla pod/bean
450 g/3$\frac{1}{2}$ cups old-fashioned rolled oats
300 g/2$\frac{1}{4}$ cups barley or millet flakes
50 g/$\frac{1}{2}$ cup soy bran
$\frac{1}{2}$ teaspoon ground ginger
70 g/$\frac{2}{3}$ cup pumpkin seeds
70 g/$\frac{2}{3}$ cup sunflower seeds
70 g/1 cup rice puffs (brown or white)
90 g/$\frac{2}{3}$ cup chopped dried fruit, such as apricots, cranberries, figs, raspberries, or a combination
plain/natural yogurt, to serve

a large sterilized glass jar with an airtight lid

Serves 30–40

Preheat the oven to 120°C (250°F) Gas $\frac{1}{2}$. Put the honey in a cup and stir in the vanilla paste or seeds. In a separate bowl, mix together the oats, barley or millet flakes, soya/soy bran and ginger together. Line a baking sheet with baking paper and spread out the granola mixture over it. Drizzle the honey mixture over the granola as evenly as possible, trying to cover it all. Bake for about 10 minutes, or until it is a light golden colour.

Tip the granola into a bowl and stir in the rest of the ingredients. Once cooled, store in an airtight jar. The granola should keep for at least 1 month.

Soft polenta is like porridge in that everyone has their favourite way of serving it; with cold milk, with hot cocoa or like here with yogurt. Sprinkle a spoonful of roasted and salted sesame seeds on top and enjoy! This breakfast will keep your tummy happy for many hours.

Soft polenta with yogurt and sesame seeds

1/2 teaspoon sea salt
170 g/1 cup coarse polenta/
   cornmeal
500 g/2 cups plain/natural yogurt
4 tablespoons sesame seeds

*a sterilized glass jar with an
   airtight lid (optional)*

Serves 2

Bring 840 ml/3 1/2 cups water to a boil, add the salt and slowly whisk in the polenta. Lower the heat, cover, and let cook for 15 minutes. There's no need to stir. Remove from the heat and leave it to rest, covered, for another 15 minutes. If you prefer harder polenta, use 750 ml/3 cups of water.

While the polenta is cooking, prepare the sesame seeds. Put them in a sieve/strainer and rinse quickly under running water. Drain well. Wetting sesame seeds not only rinses off possible dust, but also prevents the seeds from jumping out of your pan and from burning. Put the sesame seeds in a heavy-bottomed frying pan/skillet over medium heat and dry-roast, stirring constantly up and down, until the seeds puff up and become golden. You can dry-roast sesame seeds in advance – stored in a sealed jar when cooled they will keep for 1 month.

Scoop the polenta onto 2 separate plates, pour over the yogurt and sprinkle with sesame seeds. Enjoy your breakfast!

Using fresh, seasonal ingredients simply prepared is the secret of any good recipe, including this one. Sometimes referred to as continental lentils, the hearty disc-shaped pulses used here do not disintegrate when cooked so make an ideal ingredient for rustic soups and casseroles. For a more substantial soup, add diced chicken breast along with the Swiss chard and let it gently poach in the stock, until just cooked through and tender.

Brown lentil and Swiss chard soup

1 litre/4 cups vegetable or chicken stock
280 g/1 1/2 cups dried brown lentils
65 ml/1/4 cup olive oil
1 onion, chopped
4 garlic cloves, finely chopped
850 g/1 lb. 14 oz. Swiss chard, trimmed and thinly sliced
65 ml/1/4 cup freshly squeezed lemon juice
leaves from a small bunch of fresh coriander/cilantro, roughly chopped
sea salt and freshly ground black pepper, to taste

Serves 4

Put the stock and lentils in a large saucepan and bring to the boil. Reduce the heat to medium and cook for 1 hour, uncovered, until the lentils are tender. Reduce the heat to low.

Heat the oil in a large frying pan set over high heat. Add the onion and garlic along with a pinch of salt. Cook for 4–5 minutes, stirring often, until softened.

Stir in the Swiss chard and stir-fry for 2–3 minutes, until wilted. Add the chard mixture to the lentils and cook over low heat for 10 minutes.

Stir in the lemon juice and coriander and season to taste with salt and pepper. Serve immediately.

This is a substantial soup that combines the sweetness of peppers with the heat of chilli/chile in the accompanying salsa. It can be made using canned black beans but the flavour of the soup will be less pronounced.

Cuban black bean and red pepper soup

200 g/1 cup dried
   black beans, soaked
   overnight, or the
   contents of 2 ×
   400-g/14-oz. cans,
   drained
1 small onion, peeled
1 small green (bell)
   pepper, cut in half
   and deseeded
1 bay leaf
sea salt and caster/
   granulated sugar,
   to taste
crème fraîche or sour
   cream, to serve

Sofrito

3 tablespoons olive oil
2 garlic cloves, chopped
1 onion, roughly chopped
4 red or yellow (bell)
   peppers, 2 deseeded
   and chopped and 2 cut
   in half and deseeded
1 teaspoon ground cumin
1 teaspoon dried
   oregano

1 bay leaf
1/2 tablespoon red wine
   vinegar

Salsa

1–2 hot red chillies/chiles,
   stalks removed and
   deseeded
1 shallot, chopped
3 garlic cloves, peeled
2 tablespoons white wine
   vinegar
4 ripe tomatoes, skinned
   and chopped
1/2 teaspoon ground
   cumin
1/2 teaspoon dried
   oregano
2 tablespoons chopped
   fresh coriander/cilantro
sea salt and caster/
   granulated sugar,
   to taste

Serves 4–6

In a large saucepan, add the beans with all of their other ingredients and 1 litre/4 cups of water, cover and bring to the boil, then turn down the heat and simmer for about 1 1/2 hours, or until soft. If using canned beans, cook for only 30 minutes. When they are cooked, discard the onion, (bell) pepper and bay leaf, then transfer a ladleful of beans to a bowl and mash them.

While the beans are cooking, make the sofrito. Heat the oil in another pan and fry the garlic for a few seconds, then tip in the onion and chopped red or yellow (bell) peppers and fry over low heat until soft. Add the cumin, oregano and bay leaf and cook for a few minutes together.

Put the halved red or yellow (bell) peppers directly over a gas flame or under a grill/broiler, skin-side towards the heat source. When the skin is blackened all over, put the peppers in a food bag for a few minutes. Take them out, remove the skin and chop the flesh.

Stir the mashed beans into the sofrito. Add the remaining cooked beans with their liquid and stir in the vinegar, sugar and salt (about 1/2 teaspoon of sugar and 1 teaspoon of salt should be just about right). Combine the skinned and chopped red or yellow (bell) peppers with the rest of the soup and simmer everything together for a few minutes.

For the salsa, in a food processor, pulse the chilli/chile, shallot, garlic and vinegar to a purée. Add the chopped tomatoes, cumin and herbs and pulse again briefly. Season with salt and sugar to taste.

Serve the soup with a dollop of crème fraîche or sour cream and one of salsa.

Spelt is such a filling, wholesome grain and it has an excellent bite to it. If you are not a fan of spelt, you can use rye grains instead. Enjoy this as a bowl as it comes or as a side salad to another dish.

Artichoke salad with spelt grains

150 g/1 cup dried spelt grains
2 × 250 g/9 oz. cans of artichoke hearts, drained
150 g/5½ oz. feta cheese, chopped into cubes
½ bunch spring onions/scallions, sliced diagonally
2 tablespoons chopped fresh flat-leaf parsley
4–5 tablespoons flaked/slivered almonds, toasted
sea salt and freshly ground black pepper, to taste
freshly squeezed lemon juice, to taste
olive oil, for drizzling

Serves 2–4

If soaking the grains overnight (I'd recommend this if you have time as it allows for a more even texture throughout), place them in double the amount of water.

The next day, drain and rinse the grains. Place in a large saucepan with a good pinch of salt and boil for approximately 22–25 minutes, or until tender but still al dente. If you haven't pre-soaked the grains, extend the cooking time by around 20 minutes. Drain and allow to cool completely.

Slice the artichoke hearts into large bite-sized pieces. Place in a bowl and add the sliced spring onions/scallions, feta and parsley.

Fold in the spelt grains, season to taste and fold in the toasted almond flakes.

Season with salt, pepper and a squeeze of lemon juice and a drizzle of good oil.

The savoury granola adds a nutritious, nutty crunch to this salad. It's worth making double the quantity to eat as a snack or perhaps sprinkle over yogurt for breakfast. If serving on sweet dishes, simply omit the tamari sauce and store any leftover granola in an airtight container.

Mixed leaves with savoury granola

150 g/5 oz. mixed salad leaves
2 nectarines, halved, stoned/pitted
   and sliced
125 g/4¼ oz. mozzarella, drained
   and torn into pieces
3 tablespoons extra virgin olive oil
freshly squeezed juice of ½ lemon
sea salt and freshly ground black
   pepper, to taste

Savoury granola

1 tablespoon buckwheat groats
1 tablespoon shelled hemp seeds
2 tablespoons sunflower seeds
2 tablespoons pumpkin seeds
a large handful of blanched
   almonds
1½ teaspoons tamari or light
   soy sauce
1½ teaspoons clear honey

Serves 4

To make the savoury granola, toast the buckwheat and hemp seeds in a large, dry frying pan/skillet over medium heat for 2–3 minutes, tossing the pan regularly, until they start to smell toasted. Transfer to a bowl and add the sunflower and pumpkin seeds to the pan. Toast the seeds, again tossing the pan regularly, for 4–5 minutes, until starting to turn golden, then add to the bowl. Finally, add the almonds to the pan and toast for 5 minutes, turning occasionally, until starting to colour. Roughly chop the nuts and add to the bowl with the seeds.

Add the tamari and honey to the nuts and seeds and stir until combined, then leave to cool.

Meanwhile, place the salad leaves in a large serving dish and add the nectarines and mozzarella. Drizzle the olive oil and lemon juice over and season with salt and pepper. Gently toss the salad and sprinkle the granola over before serving.

Fragrant spices have multiple health benefits and this North African-influenced dish is a great way to introduce a sweetness that negates the craving for dessert. You can easily purchase a *ras el hanout* spice blend or make your own, as below, to coat the protein- and mineral-rich amaranth and chickpeas.

Moroccan pumpkin stew

2 tablespoons coconut or olive oil
1 red onion, chopped
2 garlic cloves, chopped
4 teaspoons *ras el hanout*
  (see Note)
225 g/1 cup amaranth
200 g/1½ cups dried chickpeas/
  garbanzo beans, soaked overnight
  in cold water
1 large sweet potato, cubed
1 pumpkin – you will need
  735g/1lb. 10 oz. cubed flesh
¼ teaspoon sea salt
65 g/½ cup raisins
90 g/1 cup toasted flaked/slivered
  almonds
sea salt and freshly ground
  black pepper, to taste
sprigs of coriander/cilantro,
  to garnish (optional)

*a sterilized glass jar with an
  airtight lid (optional)*

Serves 4

Gently heat the oil in a large pan, add the onion, garlic, and spice and sweat over low heat for 5 minutes.

Meanwhile, put the amaranth into a pan with 500 ml/2 cups of water. Bring to the boil, then simmer for 20 minutes. Take off the heat and allow any remaining water to be absorbed.

Drain the chickpeas/garbanzo beans and add with the chopped sweet potato and pumpkin to the pan containing the onions. Add 750 ml/3 cups of water, cover and simmer for 15 minutes. Stir thoroughly, then add the salt and raisins and simmer for a further 5 minutes.

Season the amaranth to taste and stir in three-quarters of the almonds. Serve with the pumpkin stew, garnished with the remaining almonds and sprigs of coriander/cilantro.

Note: To make your own *ras el hanout* spice mix, in a dry pan toast 3 tablespoons cumin seeds, 2½ tablespoons coriander seeds, 1½ tablespoons ground cinnamon, 2½ teaspoons ground ginger, 2 teaspoons black peppercorns, 1½ teaspoons ground turmeric, 1 teaspoon paprika, ½ teaspoon cardamom seeds, ½ teaspoon ground nutmeg, ¼ teaspoon cloves and a pinch of saffron threads for a few minutes until fragrant. Grind in a spice grinder or clean coffee grinder with a few dried rose petals. Store any leftover spice mixture in an airtight jar.

You will feel your body relaxing and your stomach thanking you while you eat this stew! It's made with only a couple of ingredients, the consistency is rich and creamy and the taste slightly sweet. After travelling, not eating well or a stressful day, this stew will take all your worries away!

Healing adzuki bean stew with amaranth

200 g/1 cup dried adzuki beans
180 g/1 1/2 cups peeled, seeded
   and cubed Hokkaido or
   kabocha pumpkin
70 g/1/3 cup amaranth
2 tablespoons soy sauce
1/2 tablespoon umeboshi vinegar
1/2 teaspoon ground turmeric
1/2 teaspoon sea salt

Serves 2–3

Cover the adzuki beans with 1 litre/quart of water in a saucepan and soak overnight (this is not necessary but will speed up the cooking). Bring them to a boil in the soaking water, then add the pumpkin and cook, half-covered, over low heat until the adzuki are half-done (about 30 minutes). Add the amaranth and cook until both the adzuki and amaranth are soft (another 20–30 minutes). Season with the remaining ingredients and adjust the thickness by adding hot water, if necessary.

This stew doesn't have any oil and provides the body with a lot of well-balanced nutrients. It is a great winter dish when you feel exhausted and need comfort food that is easy to digest.

Having a plate full of lively colours every day of the week keeps you healthy from the inside out! Even if you don't really like raw beetroot/beet, there is only a small amount here that can barely be tasted, but it gives the bowl an amazingly vibrant pink colour and colour equals goodness!

Pink quinoa salad with fennel and arame

170 g/1 cup quinoa
130 g/1 1/3 cups thinly sliced
  fennel bulb
3 tablespoons freshly squeezed
  lemon juice
20 g/1 cup dried arame strips
1 teaspoon tamari sauce
1/2 small beetroot/beet, finely
  grated
1 tablespoon umeboshi vinegar
3 tablespoons sesame oil
3 spring onions/scallions,
  finely chopped
2 tablespoons dry-roasted
  sunflower seeds (optional)
sea salt, to taste

Serves 2

In a saucepan, bring 400 ml/1 3/4 cups of water to a boil.

Wash the quinoa, drain it well and add it to the boiling water together with 1/4 teaspoon salt. Lower the heat, cover and let simmer for 20 minutes or until the water is completely absorbed and then turn off the heat.

Place the sliced fennel in a bowl, add 2 tablespoons of the lemon juice and 1/2 teaspoon salt and squeeze well with your hands, until the fennel starts 'sweating'.

To cook the arame, put the strips in a small saucepan, add 450 ml/2 cups of water and let boil, uncovered. Lower the heat, half-cover and cook for 15 minutes. Drain off the excess water, add the tamari and quickly stir over low heat until it is absorbed.

In a large salad bowl, mix the grated beet(root) with the vinegar, which helps to accentuate the bright pink colour. Add the cooked quinoa, the remaining lemon juice, 4 tablespoons cooked arame and the oil. Just before serving, mix in the fennel and spring onions/scallions. Taste and season with some more salt and lemon juice if necessary. To add extra texture to this salad, sprinkle the dry-roasted sunflower seeds over it.

Using peas, which contain an amazing 13% protein, instead of chickpeas to make these falafel mean they are a lot easier to digest. If you want to start your kids on eating green things, or if you just want to add some more into your own diet, these falafel are a great transition food, full of guilty delicious taste and good-for-you greens! The key to an authentic tabbouleh is to chop your ingredients (particularly the parsley) as finely as possible.

Hemp tabbouleh with pea and mint falafel

Hemp tabbouleh

80 g/2 cups fresh flat-leaf parsley, finely chopped
10 g/¼ cup fresh mint, finely chopped
a handful of finely chopped kale
1 large tomato, finely diced
½ white onion, finely diced
a 10-cm/4-inch piece of cucumber, finely diced
freshly squeezed juice of 1 lemon
2½ tablespoons olive oil, plus extra for the falafel
4 tablespoons hemp seeds
2 heaped tablespoons pomegranate seeds
sea salt, to taste

Pea and mint falafel

150 g/1 cup cooked peas
10 g/¼ cup fresh mint, chopped
1 garlic clove
4 tablespoons chopped spring onion/scallion
¼ teaspoon bicarbonate of/baking soda
2 teaspoons freshly squeezed lemon juice

Lemon tahini sauce

115 g/⅓ cup light tahini
1 tablespoon freshly squeezed lemon juice

a baking sheet, lined with foil and greased

Serves 2

Toss the chopped parsley, mint and kale together in a large mixing bowl, then add the tomato, onion and cucumber. Pour in the lemon juice and olive oil and mix well. Add the hemp and pomegranate seeds and season with salt. Set aside.

Preheat the oven to 200°C (400°F) Gas 6.

Combine all of the falafel ingredients in a food processor and pulse until well incorporated, but still have a little texture.

Divide the mixture into 6–8 pieces and roll each one into a ball. Put on the prepared baking sheet, then press down gently in the centre of each ball to form an indent.

Lightly brush the tops of the falafel with olive oil. Bake in the preheated oven for 15 minutes, flip the falafel over and bake for another 10 minutes.

Meanwhile, to make the sauce, mix the tahini and lemon juice together with 1 tablespoon of water, using a whisk.

Serve the warm pea and mint falafel on a bed of hemp tabbouleh and drizzled with the lemon tahini sauce.

Asian cuisine makes the perfect bowl food. In this Asian-inspired salad, the sesame seeds form a thick, nutty crust around slices of tamari-marinated tofu, which are then served on top of an adzuki bean and pea shoot salad.

Sesame-coated tofu with adzuki beans

450 g/1 lb. tofu, drained, patted dry
  and sliced into 8 slices about
  1 cm/½ inch thick
2 tablespoons tamari or light
  soy sauce
4 heaped teaspoons cornflour/
  cornstarch
6 heaped tablespoons sesame
  seeds
125 g/4¼ oz. canned adzuki beans,
  drained and rinsed
11-cm/4-inch piece cucumber,
  quartered lengthways and
  thinly sliced
3 spring onions/ scallions, thinly
  sliced diagonally
120 g/4 oz. pea shoots and mixed
  leaves
2 handfuls of sugar snap peas,
  sliced diagonally
1 red chilli/chile, seeded and
  thinly sliced
sunflower oil, for frying

Dressing

2 tablespoons tamari or light
  soy sauce
2 tablespoons freshly squeezed
  lime juice
1 teaspoon caster/ superfine sugar
1-cm/½-inch piece fresh root
  ginger, peeled and finely chopped

Serves 4

Put the tofu in a shallow dish and pour the tamari over. Turn the tofu to coat it in the tamari and leave to marinate for 1 hour, spooning the tamari over the tofu occasionally.

Mix together the cornflour/cornstarch and sesame seeds in a second shallow dish. Add the tofu in batches and turn until evenly coated in the mixture. Pour enough sunflower oil into a large frying pan/skillet to shallow-fry the tofu. Fry the tofu over medium heat in two batches for 2–3 minutes on each side until golden, then drain on paper towels.

Meanwhile, mix together all the ingredients for the dressing and stir to dissolve the sugar.

Put the adzuki beans, cucumber, two of the spring onions/scallions, the pea shoots and mixed leaves, sugar snap peas and half the chilli/chile in a large serving dish. Pour enough of the dressing over to coat and toss gently until combined.

Pile the sesame-coated tofu on top of the salad and sprinkle over the remaining spring onions/scallions and chilli/chile.

Chimichurri, the feisty Argentinian version of pesto, makes a great base for a salad dressing. You'll have some left over so just keep it in a jar in the fridge for up to 2 weeks. It's great poured over pasta, noodles, rice or beans, as here.

Black bean bowl with chimichurri dressing

2 red-fleshed sweet potatoes, peeled and cut into bite-sized cubes
2 red (bell) peppers, quartered and deseeded
100 g/3¾ oz. rocket/arugula leaves
a 400-g/14-oz. can of black beans, drained and rinsed
4 tablespoons pumpkin seeds, toasted

Chimichurri dressing

15 g/½ oz. flat-leaf parsley, finely chopped
8 g/¼ oz. oregano leaves, finely chopped
1 large garlic clove, crushed
freshly squeezed juice of ½ lemon
1 red chilli/chile, deseeded and finely chopped
6 tablespoons extra virgin olive oil, plus extra for brushing
sea salt and freshly ground black pepper, to taste

Serves 4

Preheat the oven to 200°C (400°F) Gas 6.

Brush the sweet potatoes with olive oil and roast in a roasting pan in the preheated oven for 35–40 minutes, turning once, until tender.

Meanwhile, brush both sides of the red (bell) peppers with olive oil and arrange on a baking sheet. Roast for 35 minutes, turning once, or until tender and blackened in places. Put the peppers in a bowl and cover with clingfilm/plastic wrap; this will make them easier to peel.

While the sweet potatoes and (bell) peppers are roasting, make the chimichurri dressing. Put the parsley, oregano, garlic, lemon juice, chilli/chile and olive oil in a food processor or blender, season, and process until coarsely chopped. (The mixture can also be chopped by hand.) Set aside.

Peel off the skin of the (bell) peppers and cut into bite-sized pieces. Arrange the rocket/arugula leaves on 4 serving plates and top with the sweet potatoes, black beans and red (bell) pepper. Spoon enough of the dressing over the salad to lightly coat it and sprinkle the pumpkin seeds on top before serving.

An excellent, lighter alternative to pasta, spaghetti squash is full of fibre and low in carbohydrates. The pesto is packed with chlorophyll-containing ingredients, including vitamin- and mineral-rich nori. This works well with the tofu to create a satisfying protein-based bowl.

Spaghetti squash with tofu, nori and kale pesto

1 large spaghetti squash
100 ml/½ cup olive, plus
  2 tablespoons
½ teaspoon sea salt
1 teaspoon dried Italian
  herbs (such as a
  mixture of thyme,
  oregano, marjoram
  and rosemary)
400 g/14 oz. smoked or
  herb-marinated tofu
35 g/¼ cup pine nuts,
  plus extra toasted to
  garnish

35 g/1¼ oz. kale
10 g/⅓ oz. dried green
  nori (sheets or
  sprinkles)
35 g/1¼ oz. basil
freshly squeezed juice
  of ½ lemon
2 garlic cloves
2 tablespoons shelled
  hemp seeds
freshly ground black
  pepper, to taste

Serves 4

Preheat the oven to 220°C (425°F) Gas 7.

Prepare the squash by slicing in half lengthwise. Scoop out the seeds and the central flesh. Put both halves on a baking sheet, hollow side up, and drizzle over 2 tablespoons of olive oil, plus salt and pepper to taste. Scatter the dried herbs over the squash (if you prefer to use fresh herbs, chop finely before adding). Roast in the preheated oven for 35 minutes.

Meanwhile, prepare the tofu by draining it, then wrapping in paper towels. Put between two chopping boards, weigh it down (such as with heavy food cans), and leave for 10 minutes until pressed firm.

Dry-roast the pine nuts in a pan over medium heat, tossing until brown on all sides. Put in a food processor with the kale, nori (tear into smaller pieces if using the sheets), basil, lemon juice, garlic cloves, hemp seeds, and the remaining olive oil and process until the pesto reaches a coarse consistency.

Slice the tofu 5-mm/¼-inch thick, put on a non-stick baking sheet, and roast in the oven for 8–10 minutes.

Use a fork to scrape the flesh of the squash into spaghetti strands, toss with the pesto and tofu, and serve on warmed plates. Season to taste with black pepper and garnish with extra toasted pine nuts.

This Egyptian-inspired stew is both tasty and filling. Lentils and rice are cooked together to cut down on the cooking stages; the rice is fermented and the lentils soaked to make this delicious dish easier to digest.

Koshari bowl

50 g/¼ cup short-grain brown rice
50 g/¼ cup sweet brown rice
2 tablespoons yogurt whey or kefir whey
100 g/½ cup green or brown lentils
small piece of kombu seaweed (optional)
2 dried bay leaves
100 ml/scant ½ cup olive oil
240 g/2 full cups onion, cut into thin half-moons
½ teaspoon sea salt
110 g/1 full cup carrots, cut into matchsticks
¼ teaspoon ground cinnamon
⅛ teaspoon chilli/chili powder
¾ teaspoon cumin seeds, crushed
4 whole cloves
3 tablespoons soy sauce
1 tablespoon apple cider vinegar
3 tablespoons flat-leaf parsley, chopped
a 720-ml/24-oz. capacity sterilized glass jar with an airtight lid

Serves 3

Mix both rices together, wash, drain, put in a clean glass jar and cover with 240 ml/1 cup of water. Add the whey, stir and cover with muslin/cheesecloth or a paper towel. Let the mixture ferment at room temperature for at least 24 hours, but ideally 2–3 days (if fermenting for over 24 hours in the summer, put the mixture in the fridge, though). Discard the soaking water.

Wash the lentils and soak them at room temperature for 24 hours in the preserving jar covered with 480 ml/2 cups of water. Loosely cover the jar with a lid or with muslin/cheesecloth with a rubber band tied around it.

Combine the soaked rice, lentils and reserved lentil soaking water in a saucepan. Pour over 1.2 litres/5 cups of water, add the kombu (if using) and the bay leaves. Bring to the boil, lower the heat and cover. Cook for 35–40 minutes. There should be enough water to make a thick stew. If it's too thick, add a little more hot water while cooking.

Meanwhile, prepare the vegetables. Heat the oil in a frying pan/skillet, add the onions and ¼ teaspoon of salt and mix well over medium heat. Add the carrots and another ¼ teaspoon of salt and mix again. Lower the heat to its minimum setting and sauté for 10 minutes, covered. Add the cinnamon, chilli powder, crushed cumin seeds and cloves, stir well and continue to sauté for another 15 minutes, until completely soft, creamy and slightly caramelized. Pour in the soy sauce and vinegar, stir and sauté for another 2 minutes.

When the rice and lentils are soft and creamy, add two-thirds of the sautéed vegetables to the saucepan containing the lentils and mix well to get a thick stew. Taste and adjust the seasoning if necessary and add the chopped parsley. Serve in bowls or soup plates and divide the leftover sautéed vegetables among the portions. Enjoy with a slice of sourdough or kefir bread and a bowl of greens!

Note: Whey is a by-product of homemade yogurt, the liquid that pools on top and can be drained for use in this recipe.

Yota is a typical Istrian stew, also popular in some parts of Slovenia and northern Italy. The main ingredients are borlotti beans and sauerkraut, which makes this a strong and filling winter dish. Another ingredient that is never omitted by Istrian nonnas is spare ribs, so if you want to get the authentic smell and taste of yota, make sure you add them. For vegan yota, a piece of smoked tofu can be added instead, but only at the end of cooking. Avoid adding all the sauerkraut at once, but leave a third of the amount to add when the stew is ready, in order to benefit from live cultures in the sauerkraut that are de-activated with cooking.

Yota

340 g/2 cups dried borlotti beans
3 dried bay leaves
1 small dried chilli/chile
1 strip kombu seaweed (optional)
200 g/6½ oz. spare ribs or smoked tofu
2 small potatoes (around 210 g/ 7½ oz. total weight)
300 g/1½ cups sauerkraut
2 garlic cloves, crushed
2 tablespoons olive oil
1 teaspoon sweet paprika
½ teaspoon sea salt
1 vegetable stock/bouilllon cube
freshly ground black pepper, to taste

a pressure cooker (optional)

Serves 4

Soak the beans in 2.4 litres/10 cups of water for 24 hours. Bring the beans to the boil in the soaking water, and then discard the water. Put the drained beans, bay leaves, chilli, kombu, spare ribs (if using) and 1.7 litres/ 7 cups of water in the pressure cooker. Securely close the lid, put on high heat and wait for the pressure to rise. Lower the heat to a minimum and cook for 45 minutes. If you are not using a pressure cooker, cook in a saucepan with a matching lid, covered, until the beans get soft, adding a little extra water during cooking, if necessary.

Meanwhile, peel and cut potatoes into quarters. If you are using tofu/ seitan instead of spare ribs, cut into small cubes.

If using a pressure cooker, wait for the pressure to come down, and open the lid. Remove the bay leaves, take out the kombu (if using), chop it and put it back into the pot. Add the potatoes, 200 g/1 cup of the sauerkraut and smoked tofu (if using) and cook covered (not under pressure) for 20 minutes. Take out the potatoes and press them through a potato ricer or mash them with a fork. Return to the pot. Add sweet paprika, freshly ground black pepper, the vegetable stock cube and salt and bring to the boil.

Turn off the heat and add the remaining 100 g/½ cup of sauerkraut, crushed garlic and olive oil. Taste and adjust the seasoning if necessary. The stew should be creamy and thick. If too dense, add a little more water.

Ideally, yota should sit covered for at least 30 minutes before serving, but if you're in a hurry you can serve it immediately. Leftovers are very tasty the next day, or even the second day after cooking.

VIBRANT VEGETABLES

This recipe is great for those following a cleansing anti-candida and parasitic diet, which is great to do during the spring months. Greens form the bulk of the diet which makes this soup easily digestible. It's a fantastic way to get essential nutrients. Chlorella, an algae, is a great source of iron and Vitamins B6 and B12 and is immune boosting, which makes it excellent to use during a detox.

Super spring greens soup

1 head of broccoli
200 g/7 oz. spring/collard greens
50 g/1 cup chopped watercress, plus extra to garnish
750 ml/3¼ cups hot vegan stock (made from stock cubes or bouillon cubes/powder)
1 teaspoon chlorella powder
½ teaspoon freshly ground black pepper
3–4 tablespoons mixed seeds

Serves 3-4

Chop the broccoli and greens. Steam for 5–10 minutes until lightly cooked using either an electric steamer or a colander set over a pan of boiling water, covered with a lid.

Transfer the steamed vegetables to a large mixing bowl and add the watercress. Pour in the hot stock and use a hand blender to combine. Once you have a smooth soup, stir in the chlorella powder and season with black pepper. Serve immediately, garnished with the mixed seeds and extra watercress.

Note: As with many supernutrients, chlorella will lose some of its benefits if overheated, hence adding it at the last minute after the soup has cooled slightly during blending.

This bowl of soup tastes amazingly creamy without using any cream. The trick is to use a generous amount of the cauliflower and using a good quality food processor to purée it to the right consistency. Another trick is to use a little coconut milk, which can fool any dairy lover. Warning, you may end up snacking on the roasted pumpkin seeds before they make it into the soup as a garnish!

Cauliflower soup with roasted pumpkin seeds

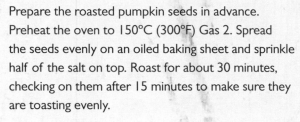

30 g/¼ cup pumpkin seeds
2 teaspoons Himalayan salt
1 medium onion, chopped
1 tablespoon olive oil
3 garlic cloves, chopped
1 large head cauliflower (cut into small florets)

1 tablespoon butter
700 ml/3 cups vegetable stock
120 ml/½ cup unsweetened light coconut milk

Serves 4–6

Prepare the roasted pumpkin seeds in advance. Preheat the oven to 150°C (300°F) Gas 2. Spread the seeds evenly on an oiled baking sheet and sprinkle half of the salt on top. Roast for about 30 minutes, checking on them after 15 minutes to make sure they are toasting evenly.

In a large saucepan or pot, fry the onion in olive oil over medium–high heat for about 5 minutes or until translucent. Lower the heat slightly, add the garlic, and fry for another minute or so. Remove from the heat.

In a separate frying pan/skillet, fry half of the cauliflower in the butter. Cook until the cauliflower is toasted. Transfer the cooked cauliflower into a bowl and set aside. Repeat the cooking process with the rest of the cauliflower – this prevents overcrowding in the pan to make sure all the ingredients are cooked evenly.

Once your cauliflower is cooked add it all to the pan of fried onion and garlic with 480 ml/2 cups of water, remaining salt and vegetable stock. Bring to the boil, then cover and simmer for 30 minutes. Remove from the heat and stir in the coconut milk.

Purée the soup in a food processor. Return to the heat and warm through. To serve, ladle the soup into bowls and garnish with the pumpkin seeds.

If you've never had soup for breakfast, you should try treating yourself with a bowl of hot miso soup like this one. In Japan, miso soup is traditionally served for breakfast, accompanied by rice and pickled vegetables. It's very clear why the Japanese have the world's longest life expectancy! Apart from nourishing you with enzymes, vitamins and minerals, this delicious, energizing soup will also support your immune system – perfect if you're suffering from fatigue or the common cold. In warmer weather, you may want to substitute darker miso pastes with the milder sweet white miso.

Healing miso soup

7-cm/3-inch piece dried wakame
(seaweed)
2-cm/1-inch piece fresh ginger
4 spring onions/scallions
110 g/2/3 cup fresh tofu
2 tablespoons sesame oil
4 garlic cloves, crushed
pinch of sea salt
480 ml/2 cups hot water
1–2 tablespoons barley or rice
miso
2 tablespoons fresh flat-leaf parsley,
chopped
freshly squeezed juice of 1/2 lemon

Serves 2

Soak the wakame in a bowl with 120 ml/1/2 cup of cold water until soft. Drain (reserve the water), cut into small pieces and set aside. Peel the fresh ginger and finely mince half of it. Finely grate the other half in a small bowl and keep for later. Chop the spring onions/scallions and cut the tofu into small cubes.

In a frying pan/skillet, sauté the white part of the spring onions/scallions for 1 minute in the sesame oil, then add the garlic, ginger and salt. Sauté a little longer, add the hot water, tofu and set-aside wakame and cover. Bring to the boil, then lower the heat and simmer for 4 minutes. Remove from the heat.

Pour approximately 60 ml/1/4 cup of hot water into a small bowl. Add the miso and purée really well with a fork, until completely dissolved. Pour back, cover and let sit for 2–3 minutes. Take the grated ginger in your hand and squeeze it to release the juice directly into the hot soup. Discard the remaining ginger pulp. Add the chopped spring onion/scallion greens, parsley and lemon juice and serve immediately!

A hearty combination of Mediterranean flavours can be found in this vibrant salad bowl. Choose a combination of different tomatoes to add colour and flavour and experiment with different flavoured herbs. Baking and then grilling/broiling the feta gives it a fabulous crispy coating and creamy centre.

Heirloom tomato and griddled feta on orzo with lemon dressing

100 g/½ cup orzo (risoni)
3 tablespoons extra virgin olive oil
grated zest and freshly squeezed
  juice of 1 lemon
1½ tablespoons clear honey
1 small garlic, crushed
25–30 g/1 cup rocket/arugula
  leaves (handful)
a 400-g/14-oz. can chickpeas,
  drained
350 g/¾ lb. mixed heirloom
  tomatoes, quartered
50 g/½ cup pitted/stoned black
  olives
a handful of fresh herbs, including
  coriander, mint and basil
200 g/7 oz. feta cheese, sliced
a small roasting pan lined with foil

Serves 2

Cook the orzo in a large saucepan of lightly salted, boiling water for 6 minutes. Drain, refresh under cold water, then drain again. Transfer to a bowl and set aside.

Meanwhile, combine 2 tablespoons of the olive oil, half of the lemon zest and juice, 2 teaspoons of the honey, the garlic and salt and pepper to taste. Pour half into the cooked orzo, stir well and leave to go cold.

Preheat the oven to 190°C (375°F) Gas 5.

Put the feta in the prepared roasting pan. Drizle over the remaining olive oil, lemon zest and juice, honey and a little pepper. Bake in the preheated oven for 10 minutes.

Preheat the grill/broiler to high and put the feta underneath to cook for a further 4–5 minutes until golden. Cool for 5 minutes and then cut into quarters ready to serve.

Meanwhile, arrange the rocket/arugula, chickpeas, tomatoes, olives and herbs in serving bowls. Top each bowl with a feta quarter, drizzle over the remaining dressing and serve.

The mackerel in this vibrant salad is a wonderful source of vitamin D, protein and B vitamins. It's also a rich source of omega-3 fatty acids, a type of fat which is amazing for your health. The dressing really brings the flavour of this bowl together, as well as adding a little luxury and piquancy to your spring vegetables.

Spiralized summer salad

1 carrot
1 courgette/zucchini
10 cherry tomatoes
4 fresh basil leaves
1 sweet red (bell) pepper
1 smoked mackerel fillet, skin removed
1 tablespoon mixed sesame and pumpkin seeds

Dressing

1 tablespoon olive oil
1/2 tablespoon agave syrup
freshly squeezed juice of 1/2 lemon
1 garlic clove, finely chopped
1/2 teaspoon chilli/hot red pepper flakes
1 teaspoon vanilla extract

Serves 4

Top, tail and peel the carrot. Peel it into wide ribbons with a vegetable peeler (or use a mandolin if you have one), and do the same to the courgette/zucchini. Quarter the cherry tomatoes and finely slice the basil leaves. Cut the red (bell) pepper into thin strips. Put everything in a large mixing bowl and crumble in the mackerel fillet. Add the seeds and mix with salad servers.

To make the dressing, combine all the remaining ingredients in a small jug/pitcher and mix well. Pour this all over your salad and toss to coat everything in the dressing.

Serve with a chilled white wine. It's that easy!

Roasting cauliflower is perhaps the tastiest way of serving this humble and somewhat overlooked vegetable, especially coated in Moroccan spices and lime juice. This, with the carrots, pearl couscous and pomegranate topped with creamy labne provides a really delicious layered bowl.

Oven-roasted Romanesco cauliflower, labne and spiced nuts

250 g/9 oz. cauliflower florets
250 g/9 oz. carrots, peeled
3 tablespoons extra virgin olive oil
2 teaspoons *ras el hanout*
  (see page 43)
grated zest and freshly squeezed
  juice of 1 lime
120 g/^{2}/$_3$ cup pearl couscous
2 tablespoons chopped mixed
  herbs of your choice
50 g/^{1}/$_3$ cup pistachio nuts, toasted
  and roughly chopped
^{1}/$_2$ pomegranate
50 g/1 cup watercress leaves
100 g/^{1}/$_2$ cup creamy labne
1 tablespoon toasted sesame seeds
a little smoked paprika, to dust
sea salt and freshly ground black
  pepper, to taste

*a roasting pan lined with
  baking parchment*

Serves 2

Preheat the oven to 190°C (375°F) Gas 5.

Break the cauliflower into bite-size florets. Cut the carrots into similar size chunks. Put the cauliflower and carrots in a bowl and add 1 tablespoon of the oil, the *ras el hanout*, the grated lime zest, half of the lime juice and some salt and pepper. Toss well until evenly coated and transfer to the prepared roasting pan. Roast for 30 minutes in the preheated oven, stirring halfway through until golden and tender. Remove from the oven and leave to cool.

Bring 350 ml/1^1/$_4$ cups of water to the boil with 1 teaspoon salt. Add the couscous, return to the boil, cover and simmer gently for 10 minutes. Remove from the heat and leave undisturbed for a further 5 minutes.

Separate out the pomegranate seeds from the pomegranate over a bowl to catch all the juices. Combine the seeds, juice, remaining olive oil, remaining lime juice and season to taste. Stir into the couscous and set aside until cold.

Divide the couscous, roasted vegetables, watercress, fresh herbs and pistachio nuts between two bowls. Dollop over a spoonful of the labne and sprinkle over the sesame seeds and serve at once dusted with a little smoked paprika.

Kimchi, the highly popular Korean pickle, traditionally takes a few days to make and ferment, but with this 'cheats' version, it needs a comparatively short amount of time, just enough to let the flavours meld and mingle. This bowl contains some great textures, from the crunchy spiced kimchi to the buttery avocado.

Kimchi, avocado and alfalfa salad

2 Chinese leaves/Chinese cabbage, shredded
2 spring onions/scallions, shredded
1 red chilli/chile, seeded and diced
2.5-cm/1-inch piece fresh root ginger, peeled and very thinly sliced
2 tablespoons black sesame seeds, toasted
4 tablespoons rice vinegar
4 teaspoons caster/superfine sugar
1/2 teaspoon sea salt
2 tablespoons cold-pressed rapeseed oil
75 g/3 oz. baby spinach leaves
2 avocados, halved, stoned/pitted, peeled and sliced
2 handfuls of alfalfa sprouts

Serves 4

First make the kimchi. Mix together the Chinese leaves/Chinese cabbage, spring onions/scallions, chilli/chile, ginger, sesame seeds, rice vinegar, caster/superfine sugar and salt in a bowl and leave to sit for 30 minutes (or longer if time allows) to let the flavours develop.

Just before serving, divide the spinach and avocados between 4 serving plates, drizzle with the oil and top with the kimchi and alfalfa sprouts.

Making your own black bean sauce rather than using ready-made gives a far lighter and better result, especially as it is so often served with vegetables. You can soak or wash the black beans if you like, but for the best results cook them as they come, for added saltiness in the dish.

Sweet potato noodles with broccoli in black bean sauce

300 g/10 oz. ready-made Asian
  sweet potato vermicelli (see Tip)
3 tablespoons peanut oil
5 cm/2 inch fresh ginger, peeled
  and thinly sliced
1 red onion, sliced
250 g/4 cups broccoli
sesame seeds, toasted, to garnish

Black bean sauce

2 tablespoons doenjang
  (Korean soy bean paste)
125 ml/1/2 cup sake
60 ml/1/4 cup mirin
2 tablespoons rice wine vinegar
2 tablespoons dark soy sauce
2 teaspoons sesame oil
3 tablespoons fermented
  black beans (available online)

Serves 4

Cook the vermicelli noodles by plunging them into a large saucepan of boiling water. Return to the boil and cook for 1 minute until al dente. Drain well, refresh under cold water and shake dry. Set aside.

Next make the sauce. Whisk together the doenjang paste, sake, mirin, vinegar, soy sauce and sesame oil until smooth, then stir in the black beans. Set aside.

Heat the peanut oil in a wok or frying pan/skillet set over medium heat and fry the ginger for 10 seconds until fragrant, add the onion and stir-fry for 1 minute, then stir in the broccoli and continue to stir-fry for 1 minute, adding 1 tablespoon cold water, until the broccoli is a vibrant green.

Add the sauce and cook for 2 minutes until the broccoli is tender. Finally add the vermicelli and stir until heated through.

Serve in bowls garnished with toasted sesame seeds.

Note: Ready-made sweet potato vermicelli is available from Asian food stores or online.

Mostly used in soups and broths in Japan, soba noodles are also popular served cold in Asian-style salads. Made primarily from buckwheat, the thin noodles are coated in a light miso dressing.

Soba noodles with miso dressing

200 g/7 oz. soba noodles or
   thin egg noodles
1 carrot, cut into thirds and
   finely shredded
1 red (bell) pepper, halved, seeded
   and finely shredded
4 spring onions/ scallions,
   finely shredded
50 g/2 oz. sugar snap peas,
   thinly sliced diagonally
a handful of radishes, thinly sliced
1 red chilli/chile, seeded and
   finely chopped
1-cm/¹/₂-inch piece fresh root
   ginger, peeled and finely chopped
4 teaspoons nori flakes (optional)
1 tablespoon sesame seeds, toasted

Miso dressing

3 tablespoons mirin
3 tablespoons tamari
   or light soy sauce
3 tablespoons sweet white
   miso paste

Serves 4

Cook the noodles in plenty of salted boiling water following the pack instructions, then drain and refresh under cold running water. Drain the noodles again, leaving them to drain while you prepare the rest of the ingredients.

Meanwhile, mix together all the ingredients for the dressing.

Put the carrot, red (bell) pepper, spring onions/ scallions, sugar snap peas, radishes, chilli/chile and ginger in a serving bowl. Add the cooked noodles and dressing and toss gently but thoroughly until combined. Sprinkle with the nori flakes, if using, and sesame seeds before serving.

You would be forgiven for thinking that the only easy way to get your hands on teriyaki sauce would be to buy a bottle of the stuff in a shop. Actually, it is surprisingly easy to make yourself at home, with the added bonus of it not having any of the preservatives, sugar and flavourings that are so often added to mass-produced products. All you need is equal parts of soy sauce, mirin and sake or water, all of which are available in good supermarkets.

Teriyaki tofu with shiitake mushrooms and soba noodles

400 g/14 oz. block of firm tofu, drained
150 g/5 oz. fresh shiitake mushrooms, sliced
1 teaspoon sesame seed oil
250 g/8 oz. soba noodles
vegetable oil, for frying
4 spring onions/scallions, finely sliced
1 teaspoons toasted black or white sesame seeds

Teriyaki sauce

6 tablespoons light soy sauce (or 5 tablespoons gluten-free tamari)
6 tablespoons mirin (look for the brands made without added sugar)
6 tablespoons sake or water
1 1/2 teaspoons sesame seed oil
3 garlic cloves, chopped
4-cm/1 1/2-inch piece ginger, peeled and chopped

Serves 4

Wrap the drained tofu block in a clean dish towel, sit on a plate with a wooden board (or other weighted object) on top and leave for 20 minutes to slowly press out any excess water.

To make the teriyaki sauce, combine together the soy sauce, mirin, sake (or water), sesame seed oil, garlic and ginger in a bowl and set aside.

When the tofu has been drained, cut the block into 2.5 cm/1 inch cubes.

Put a large frying pan/skillet over high heat, add in the teriyaki sauce and all the tofu. Cook on a high heat, turning the tofu now and again for 4 minutes until the sauce has reduced a little. Turn off the heat and set to one side.

Put a large pot of water on to boil. While that is heating up, add 3 tablespoons of sunflower oil to another frying pan/skillet and put over high heat. Add in the mushrooms and fry over medium heat for 4 minutes until golden. Remove and stir into the teriyaki tofu.

Add the soba noodles to the water and cook as per the packet instructions, but test them 2 minutes before they are due to be ready – they should be just a little al dente. Drain thoroughly and add to the pan/skillet with the tofu and mushrooms and put over high heat. Toss gently until hot and the noodles have absorbed the sauce. Add in most of the sliced spring onions/scallions, then serve in bowls with the remaining spring onions/scallions and sesame seeds scattered over.

This may look like a cheat meal but there are actually a lot of healthy things in this bowl: good fats from the coconut milk, warming and stimulating spices, all mixed in with tonnes of fresh veggies and herbs. This version features all of these good parts without the unnecessary sugars that sneak into curry sauces. A suitable substitute for the white rice is jícama rice; if you can't find jícama, try making cauliflower rice in the same way.

Raw curry with jícama rice

1 large jícama/water chestnut, roughly chopped
1 tablespoon mirin (optional)
1 small courgette/zucchini, finely sliced
12 okra, finely sliced
1 large carrot, finely sliced
2 large handfuls beansprouts
1 young Thai coconut (or 400 g/2 cups full-fat coconut milk, but this isn't raw)
1 red (bell) pepper, deseeded
1 tomato
1 garlic clove
1 small Thai chilli/jalapeño
1 lemongrass stalk
1 heaped teaspoon curry powder
2 spring onions/scallions
freshly squeezed juice of 1 lime
a 2½-cm/1-inch piece of fresh ginger, plus extra grated
a large handful of fresh coriander/cilantro, plus extra to garnish

a high-speed blender

Serves 2

Begin by blending the jícama in a food processor to a fine rice-like texture. 1 large jícama should yield about 900 g/3 cups jícama rice.

Mix the jícama rice with the mirin (if using), cover and set aside.

Put the sliced courgette/zucchini, okra and carrot in a large mixing bowl with the beansprouts and set aside.

Carefully cut the coconut open, scoop out the meat and the water, and put both in a blender with the rest of the ingredients. Blend until smooth, then pour the mixture over the mixed vegetables. Mix well, cover and set aside for 2 hours at room temperature to allow the flavours to infuse and soften the vegetables before consuming.

To serve, divide the rice between two serving bowls and top with the curry mixture. Garnish with grated ginger and a sprig of coriander/cilantro and enjoy.

The heat of the chilli/chile as well as the garlicky anchovy dressing are tempered by the mild creaminess of the mozzarella and slight sweetness of the green vegetables in this simple summery salad bowl.

Mozzarella, chilli/chile and green bean bowls

200 g/7 oz. green beans, trimmed
200 g/7 oz. long-stem broccoli, trimmed
100 g/1 cup shelled peas, or frozen garden peas, defrosted
2 × 125-g/4¼-oz. balls mozzarella, drained, patted dry and torn into pieces
1 red chilli/chile, seeded and thinly sliced
a generous handful of basil leaves
sea salt and freshly ground black pepper, to taste

Dressing

5 tablespoons extra virgin olive oil
2 large garlic cloves, sliced
2 anchovy fillets in oil, drained and chopped
freshly squeezed juice of ½ lemon

Serves 4

Steam the green beans, broccoli and peas until just tender, then refresh briefly under cold running water so the vegetables remain warm.

Meanwhile, for the dressing heat the olive oil, garlic and anchovies gently in a small pan, stirring and mashing the anchovies against the side of the pan to encourage them to melt into the oil. Heat for 4 minutes until the garlic starts to colour. Stir in the lemon juice.

Arrange the vegetables on a large serving plate and top with the mozzarella and chilli/chile. Spoon enough of the dressing over to coat and toss gently. Sprinkle with basil leaves and check the seasoning, adding salt and pepper if needed.

The claypot is mostly known as a dish of Chinese origin; however, this dish is based on the Vietnamese dish, straw mushroom claypot. It's impossible to source fresh straw mushrooms in the UK, so use oyster or chestnut mushrooms instead. If you like the unusual taste and texture of straw mushrooms, you can add canned ones to the mix. For such a simple dish, this certainly packs plenty of savoury flavour too. Less than 15 minutes to prepare, this may become a popular family favourite in your house.

Mushroom claypot

½ tablespoon vegetable oil
2 garlic cloves, crushed and
    finely chopped
120 g/1 oz. whole straw
    mushrooms, drained and rinsed
    if canned
120 g/4 oz. chestnut mushrooms,
    quartered
120 g/4 oz. oyster mushrooms,
    roughly torn
4 tablespoons soy sauce or tamari
2 tablespoons soft brown sugar,
    or agave syrup
½ teaspoon salt, or to taste
1 teaspoon freshly ground
    black pepper, or to taste

To serve

steamed rice
1–2 radishes, sliced
spring onions/scallions, sliced

Serves 2–3

Put a heat-proof claypot or large pan over medium heat and add the oil. Cook the garlic for 3 minutes or until it starts to soften. Add all the mushrooms and cook for a further 1 minute, stirring.

Add all the remaining ingredients to the pan with 2–3 tablespoons of water, then cover and simmer over low heat for 10 minutes. Remove the lid and check the seasoning.

Serve with steamed rice and a simple crunchy salad of sliced radishes and spring onions/scallions.

Aubergines/eggplants play a huge role on the mezze table – there are reputed to be around 200 dishes made with them – and smoking them over a gas flame, or on a charcoal grill, is one of the most enjoyable ways of cooking and eating them. The soft, smoky-flavoured flesh is combined with other ingredients for a variety of mezze dishes, such as the well-known Lebanese and Syrian speciality, baba ghanoush. This recipe is a popular salad all over the Mediterranean region.

Smoked aubergine/eggplant and red pepper salad

2–3 large aubergines/eggplants
2 red (bell) peppers
2–3 garlic cloves, crushed
3–4 spring onions/scallions, trimmed and finely sliced
a bunch of fresh flat-leaf parsley, coarsely chopped
2–3 tablespoons olive oil
2 tablespoons pomegranate syrup/molasses, or the freshly squeezed juice of 1 lemon
sea salt and freshly ground black pepper, to taste

Serves 4–6

Put the aubergines/eggplants and (bell) peppers directly on the gas flame, or on the grid over a charcoal grill. Over the flame, the skins of the aubergines/eggplants and peppers will buckle and flake a little and will make a bit of a mess of your gas cooker but, over the charcoal grill, the skins will toughen and brown, leaving no mess! It doesn't matter which method you choose, but you are looking for the flesh of both the aubergines/eggplants and the peppers to soften, so you need to keep turning them to make sure they are evenly smoked. Once soft, pop them both into a clean, resealable plastic bag to sweat for 5 minutes, then hold them by the stalks under cold running water and peel off the skins. Squeeze out the excess water and put them on a chopping board. Remove the stalks of the aubergines/eggplants and chop the flesh to a coarse pulp. Remove the stalks and seeds of the peppers and chop the flesh to a coarse pulp as well.

Tip the pulped flesh into a bowl and add the garlic, spring onions/scallions and parsley. Season well with salt and pepper (the smoked aubergine/eggplant flesh needs salt to bring out the flavour) and bind the salad with the olive oil and pomegranate syrup/molasses or lemon juice. Drizzle a little extra pomegranate syrup/molasses over the top before serving.

MIGHTY MEAT
AND POULTRY

Mapo tofu, the Chinese minced meat and tofu dish, is also very popular in Korea, albeit with a few Korean tweaks to the ingredients. The chilli and soybean pastes used in this recipe are easy to find in an Asian market and are popping up in some supermarkets. Or, you can substitute with normal mild chilli paste and Japanese miso paste.

Korean-style mapo tofu

400 g/14 oz. tofu
sunflower oil, for frying
1 echalion/banana shallot, peeled
  and very finely chopped
1 teaspoon grated fresh ginger
1 garlic clove, crushed
350 g/12 oz. minced/ ground beef
1 tablespoon Korean gochujang
  chilli/chili paste (or other mild
  chilli/chili paste)
1 tablespoon Korean doenjang
  soybean paste (or miso paste)
freshly ground black pepper,
  to taste
175 ml/³⁄₄ cup beef or chicken
  stock
2 tablespoons mirin
2 tablespoons soy sauce
1 tablespoon coconut palm sugar
  or pure maple syrup
1¹⁄₂ teaspoons cornflour/cornstarch,
  whisked well into 2 tablespoons
  water
1 tablespoon sesame seed oil
5 chives, thinly sliced
handful of coriander/cilantro leaves
rice, to serve

Serves 4–6

Bring a pot of salted water to simmering point. Drain the tofu and cut into 2.5 cm/1 inch cubes. Carefully add the tofu to the water and simmer for 8 minutes. Then remove the tofu and leave to drain on a clean dish towel, being careful not to break the cubes.

Meanwhile, add 1 tablespoon sunflower oil to a large frying pan/ skillet and put over medium heat. When hot, add in the shallot and stir fry for 1 minute, then add in the garlic and ginger and stir-fry for another minute, being careful not to let them burn. Add in the minced/ground beef, turn up the heat a little and stir-fry for 1–2 minutes. Add in the gochujang chilli paste, the doenjang soybean paste (or miso) and a few grindings of black pepper, combine together and stir-fry on a high heat for 1–2 minutes, breaking up the beef until almost cooked.

Add in the rest of the ingredients apart from the chives, coriander/ cilantro and rice, and combine together. Gently add the drained tofu into the frying pan/skillet and carefully combine together ensuring you do not break up the tofu. Cook for 2–3 minutes until the sauce is thick and glossy.

Serve in bowls with the chives and coriander/cilantro leaves scattered over and the rice on the side.

Note: If you are avoiding refined cane sugar completely, bear in mind that most chilli/chile pastes will contain it, although the quantities of it will be very small per serving.

Chicken is an excellent source of lean protein which helps muscle growth and repair, making this salad an excellent way to repair tired arms and legs after a tough workout. It also contains an amino acid called 'tryptophan,' which increases the serotonin levels in your brain, relieving stress and enhancing your mood. Add that to the natural endorphines generated by exercise and you'll have a potent combination of things to make you smile. Chicken also contains phosphorous, which helps aid bone and teeth structure.

Spirulina green chicken salad

2 chicken breasts
sesame oil, to drizzle
3 spring onions/scallions,
   finely chopped
2 tablespoons chopped fresh
   coriander/cilantro
2 tablespoons chopped fresh mint
2 tablespoons dried fried onions
2 tablespoons toasted sesame
   seeds
cooked brown rice or a mixed
   green salad, to serve

Dressing

4 tablespoons freshly squeezed
   lime juice
1 teaspoon spirulina powder
1 tablespoon fish sauce
1 tablespoon finely chopped
   fresh ginger
2 tablespoons sweet chilli sauce

Serves 2

Preheat the oven to 180°C (350°F) Gas 4.

Drizzle the chicken breasts with sesame oil, then wrap loosely in foil. Put on a baking sheet and bake in the preheated oven for 15–20 minutes, until cooked through. Cool slightly, then pull the meat apart with your fingers to shred it and put in a large mixing bowl.

Add the spring onions/scallions, fresh coriander/cilantro, fresh mint, dried fried onions and sesame seeds to the chicken and toss together.

In a separate small bowl, whisk all the dressing ingredients together. Drizzle over the chicken salad and mix together, then serve with either cooked brown rice or a big green salad.

Fresh and fragrant, this salad is full of vibrant flavours with its sweet and sour dressing and lots of crisp vegetables. As a twist, the salad is topped with carpaccio of beef. To make the beef easier to cut into thin slices, freeze it first to firm up and use a very sharp, long-bladed knife. Choose a thick piece of beef, preferably a centre cut.

Vietnamese-style beef salad

200 g/7 oz. sirloin steak
2 handfuls of baby spinach leaves
1 carrot, sliced into thin strips
1 small cucumber, quartered
 lengthways, seeded and cut
 into thin strips
2 handfuls of finely shredded
 red cabbage
2 spring onions/scallions, thinly
 sliced diagonally
a handful of Thai basil leaves,
 roughly torn
a handful of mint leaves, roughly
 chopped
1 medium red chilli/chile, seeded
 and thinly sliced
30 g/¼ cup roasted unsalted
 peanuts, roughly chopped

Vietnamese dressing

3 tablespoons groundnut/
 peanut oil
2 tablespoons fish sauce
freshly squeezed juice of 1 lime
1 teaspoon caster/superfine sugar
sea salt and freshly ground
 black pepper, to taste

Serves 4

Put the steak in the freezer for 30 minutes to firm up and to make it easier to slice.

While the steak is in the freezer, mix together all the ingredients for the dressing and season to taste.

Divide the spinach between 4 serving plates and top with the carrot, cucumber and red cabbage. Spoon enough of the dressing over to coat and toss lightly until combined.

Remove the steak from the freezer and using a very sharp, long-bladed knife, cut into thin, elegant slices. Put the cut slices on a plate and cover with clingfilm/plastic wrap to prevent them discolouring; if you put clingfilm/plastic wrap between each layer of beef, you will be able to separate them easily.

Arrange the steak on top of the salad, season and sprinkle the spring onions/scallions, herbs, chilli/chile and peanuts over the top. Spoon more dressing over to taste, and serve immediately.

Broad beans, fresh or dried, have fed man for millennia. This recipe results in the best type of food to eat; simple, casual and flavoursome. Lamb shoulder cannot be rushed. When cooked with patience this sumptuous bowl of food will melt in your mouth.

Slow-cooked lamb salad with broad/fava beans, pomegranate and fresh mint

2 tablespoons light olive oil
1 tablespoon sea salt
1 tablespoon ground cumin
2 kg/4½ lbs. lamb shoulder
500 g/4 cups fresh young broad/fava beans
leaves from a bunch of fresh mint
about 120 g/4 oz. pomegranate seeds
2 tablespoons extra virgin olive oil
2 tablespoons freshly squeezed lemon juice
sea salt and freshly ground black pepper, to taste

a rack set over a baking tray or roasting tin

Serves 4

Preheat the oven to 160°C (325°F) Gas 3. Rub the oil then the salt and cumin all over the lamb. Sit the lamb on a rack set over a large baking tray and cook in the preheated oven for 6 hours. Remove, lightly cover with foil and let rest for up to 3 hours.

Cook the broad/fava beans in a large saucepan of boiling water for 10 minutes, until just tender. Drain well.

Use a fork or your fingers to shred the lamb off of the bone. Transfer to a bowl and add the broad/fava beans, mint, pomegranate seeds, extra virgin olive oil and lemon juice. Toss to combine, season to taste with salt and pepper and serve immediately.

Salads don't have to be restricted to the warmer summer months; this winter alternative makes a simple meal served with crusty bread. It is equally good served at room temperature for lunch, and you could use cooked beetroot/beets and canned lentils for a quick meal.

Warm ham hock, beetroot/beet and lentil salad

3 uncooked beetroot/beets, washed and each one cut into 8 wedges
4 tablespoons extra virgin olive oil
200 g/7 oz. dried green lentils
2 large garlic cloves, finely chopped
1 courgette/zucchini, quartered and diced
175 g/6 oz. vine-ripened cherry tomatoes, halved
2 tablespoons thyme leaves
2 heaped teaspoons Dijon mustard
freshly squeezed juice of 1 lemon
100 g/3¾ oz. rocket/arugula leaves
a handful of roughly chopped flat leaf parsley
180 g/6 oz. cooked smoked ham hock, shredded
sea salt and freshly ground black pepper, to taste

Serves 4

Preheat the oven to 200°C (400°F) Gas 6.

Put the beetroot/beets in a roasting pan and brush with 1 tablespoon of the olive oil. Season and bake in the preheated oven for 40–45 minutes, turning once, until tender.

Meanwhile, put the lentils in a pan and pour enough water over to cover. Bring to the boil, then turn the heat down, part-cover, and simmer for 20–25 minutes until tender, then drain.

Heat the remaining oil in a large sauté pan over medium heat and fry the garlic, courgette/zucchini and tomatoes for 3 minutes until softened. Stir in the thyme, mustard and lemon juice until combined.

Remove from the heat and fold in the rocket/arugula, parsley, ham hock and lentils, taking care not to break up the lentils, and allow the heat of the pan to wilt the leaves. Season before folding in the roasted beetroot/beets, then serve while still warm or let cool to room temperature.

Black rice has its origin in China and is a highly recommended new grain to try. It has a pleasantly mild, nutty flavour and its colour makes for striking presentation. It is also best to make this a day ahead of serving so the flavours really meld together.

Chicken soup with black forbidden rice

130 g/1 cup cooked black rice
  (see method)
2 carrots, chopped
1 celery stalk/rib, chopped
a handful of chopped fresh flat-leaf
  parsley and dill, to garnish

Chicken broth

1 chicken (cut into 8 pieces,
  bones and skin left on)
4 carrots
1 onion, peeled and quartered
1 parsnip
2 celery stalks
1 bay leaf
4 sprigs of fresh dill
a handful of chopped fresh
  flat-leaf parsley

Serves 4

Put all of the chicken broth ingredients in a large saucepan or pot on a medium–high heat. Cover with water and bring to the boil. Reduce the heat, cover and simmer for 1 hour.

Remove the white breast meat so that it doesn't overcook and set aside in the refrigerator. Return the bones to the pan and simmer for another hour. Strain the broth and chill in the refrigerator overnight.

The next day, cut or shred the chicken into bite-size pieces. Then cook the black rice according to packet instruction or using the ratio of 200 g/ 1 cup of rice to 420 ml/1³⁄₄ cups of water.

Put the rice and water in a medium saucepan or pot and bring to the boil. Reduce to a low heat, cover and simmer for 30 minutes. Remove from the heat, fluff with a fork, then put the lid back on and set aside for 5 minutes.

Skim the fat off the top of the broth and pour into a large saucepan or pot. Add in the carrots, celery and black rice. Cook for about 5 minutes or until the vegetables are tender, then add the shredded chicken and cook until heated through.

Serve immediately and garnish with chopped parsley and dill.

Despite the fact that Chinese BBQ duck is somewhat clichéd, that doesn't stop this soup from being absolutely delicious if done well. Here, to add a little fun to this soup, the duck, spring onions/scallions, cucumber and hoisin sauce form the filling for wontons. And the skin is deep fried to add a fabulous bite to the finished soup.

Dimsum duck wonton soup

½ cooked Chinese barbecue duck
1 small onion, roughly chopped
5 cm/2 inch fresh ginger, peeled, sliced and pounded
4 garlic cloves
3 whole star anise, lightly bruised
1 cinnamon stick, lightly bruised
75 ml/scant ⅓ cup shaoxing rice wine (Chinese rice wine)
75 ml/scant ⅓ cup dark soy sauce
½ cucumber, deseeded and finely chopped
2 large spring onions/ scallions, trimmed and finely chopped
2 tablespoons hoisin sauce
1 egg, beaten
24 wonton wrappers
vegetable oil, for deep frying
2 pak choi/bok choy, trimmed and thickly sliced
1 tablespoon chopped fresh coriander/cilantro

To serve

crispy duck skin
coriander/cilantro leaves

Serves 4

Remove the skin and meat from the duck and put the bones in a saucepan with 2 litres/3½ pints of cold water. Add the onion, ginger, garlic, star anise and cinnamon stick and bring to the boil over medium heat. Partially cover the pan and simmer gently for 30 minutes. Strain the stock through a fine-mesh sieve/strainer into a clean saucepan and stir in the shaoxing and soy sauce.

Meanwhile, chop the duck meat and put in a bowl with the cucumber, spring onions/scallions and hoisin sauce. Add half the beaten egg and mix to combine.

Working one at a time, lay the wonton wrappers out flat and put a tablespoon of the duck filling in the middle of each. Brush the edges with the remaining beaten egg and press together to seal.

Heat about 5 cm/2 inch oil in a wok or old saucepan until a cube of bread dropped into the oil crisps and turns brown in 20–30 seconds. Cut the duck skin into thin strips and fry in the hot oil until crispy. Remove from the pan and drain on paper towels.

Bring the duck stock to a gentle simmer, add the wontons and cook for 5 minutes. Remove with a slotted spoon and divide between serving bowls.

Add the pak choi/bok choy to the stock and simmer for 2–3 minutes until tender. Divide the pak choi/bok choy between the bowls and pour over the stock.

Serve the soup with the crispy duck skin and a few coriander/cilantro leaves sprinkled on top.

These are lovely snacks to eat while drinking beer and hanging out with friends. They can be made into a more substantial bowl by serving them with a noodle salad or turning them into fresh rolls. The betel leaves do not have much fragrance until heated, when they have their own special smell and taste – similar to cinnamon, sesame and pepper.

Lemongrass beef in betel leaves

300 g/10½ oz. rump/ round steak, very thinly sliced
1 lemongrass stalk, finely chopped
3 garlic cloves, finely chopped
1 teaspoon dried chilli/ hot red pepper flakes
1 tablespoon sugar
½ teaspoon sea salt
2½ tablespoons sesame oil
1 tablespoon sesame seeds
1 tablespoon cooking oil
1 tablespoon honey
¼ kiwi, finely chopped
150 g/5½ oz. betel leaves (or shiso/perilla), stalks removed, then washed and dried

Dipping sauce

2 Bird's Eye chillies/chiles, deseeded and finely chopped
1 garlic clove, finely chopped

1½ tablespoons caster/ granulated sugar
2 tablespoons cider vinegar
2 tablespoons fish sauce
3 tablespoons roasted salted peanuts, crushed

Noodle salad

300 g/10½ oz. thin rice vermicelli
2 carrots, shredded
½ daikon/mooli, shredded
5 tablespoons cider vinegar
5 tablespoons white sugar
lettuce leaves
Thai sweet basil
coriander/cilantro
cockscomb mint
shiso/perilla

Serves 4–6

Put the steak, lemongrass, garlic, dried chilli flakes/ hot pepper flakes, sugar, salt, 1 teaspoon of the sesame oil, the sesame seeds, cooking oil, honey and kiwi in a bowl. Mix well and rub the mixture into the steak slices. Marinate in the fridge for 20 minutes.

Preheat the oven to 180°C (350°F) Gas 4.

Put a betel leaf in front of you, shiny side up and spine pointing straight ahead and away from you. Put a couple of slices of the steak across the leaf, then roll it up as tightly as you can. The roll should be the thickness of your index finger. Put it, seam side down, in a roasting pan. Repeat this process until all the leaves and filling have been used up and arrange the rolls snugly next to each other in the pan to prevent them from unrolling. Drizzle the remaining sesame oil over the rolls and bake in the preheated oven for 12 minutes for medium–rare.

To make the dipping sauce, mix all the ingredients together in a bowl. Set aside.

To build the noodle salad, put the rice vermicelli, a pinch of salt and a dash of vinegar in a bowl or pan of boiling water, cover and allow to cook for 5–10 minutes or until soft. Drain and rinse with hot water.

Meanwhile, mix together the carrot, daikon/mooli, cider vinegar and sugar to make a pickle. Set aside for 15 minutes.

Divide the noodles between 4–6 bowls and serve with the rolls, lettuce, herbs and pickle, and dipping sauce for dipping or drizzling over the rolls.

The ingredients of this steaming hot bowl makes the presentation just as exciting as the punchy flavours inside. For a truly authentic Korean taste, seek out gochujang, which is a slightly sweet chilli/chili paste.

Bibimbap

400 g/14 oz. pork belly, chopped into thin 2.5-cm/1-inch pieces (omit if you are vegetarian)
400 g/2 cups short grain brown rice, e.g. brown sushi rice
vegetable, sunflower or rapeseed oil
2 carrots, cut into thin strips
1/2 teaspoon toasted sesame oil
1/2 teaspoon dark soy sauce
1/2 teaspoon agave syrup
150 g/5 oz. oyster or shiitake mushrooms
150 g/5 oz. beansprouts
3 onions, sliced
200 g/6½ oz. spinach leaves
4 eggs
2 spring onions/scallions, finely chopped
black sesame seeds, to sprinkle

Gochujang sauce

4 tablespoons gochujang paste
4 tablespoons toasted sesame oil
4 tablespoons dark soy sauce
2 garlic cloves, crushed
2 tablespoons agave syrup

Serves 4

To make the gochujang sauce, mix together all the ingredients. Put half the sauce over the pork belly in a bowl, cover and marinate in the fridge for at least 1 hour, or more if you have time.

Cook the rice according to the packet instructions and keep warm.

While the rice is cooking, heat 1 tablespoon oil in a pan or wok and stir-fry the carrots until beginning to soften. Add the sesame oil, soy sauce and agave syrup. Cook for 1 minute over high heat, then set aside on a plate. Cook the mushrooms, bean sprouts, onions, and spinach (which will wilt down) separately and in the same way, seasoning at the end. It is normal for the vegetables to be served at room temperature, as long as the rice, meat and eggs are hot, so don't worry about keeping them warm.

In the same pan you used for the vegetables, stir-fry the marinated pork (with the sauce it was sitting in) until cooked through. The sauce should reduce down a little with the heat, intensifying all the flavours.

In a separate pan, fry the 4 eggs however you like them – it is nice to have the yolk a little soft for this dish.

Serve the hot rice in 4 bowls and top with individual piles of vegetables and meat, finishing off with the egg in the middle and a sprinkling of spring onions/scallions and sesame seeds.

Serve with the remaining gochujang sauce, adding as much or as little as you like. The Korean way of eating this is to mix the whole thing together like crazy until all the ingredients are well combined. If it is not punchy enough, add more sauce.

There are as many recipes for meatballs in Scandinavia as there are cooks. Recipes vary regionally, both in ingredients and sizing. The homemade version is so very wholesome and worth the effort. Serve with creamy mashed potato.

Real Swedish meatballs

30 g/^{1}/$_3$ cup porridge/old-fashioned oats or breadcrumbs
150 ml/^{2}/$_3$ cup meat stock (chicken works well, too)
400 g/14 oz. minced/ground beef
250 g/9 oz. minced/ground pork (minimum 10% fat)
1 UK medium/US large egg
2^1/$_2$ tablespoons plain/all-purpose flour
pinch of sea salt
1 teaspoon ground allspice
^{1}/$_2$ teaspoon ground black pepper
^{1}/$_2$ teaspoon ground white pepper
a dash of Worcestershire sauce or soy sauce
1 small onion, grated
butter and oil, for frying
mashed potato, to serve

Stirred lingonberries

250 g/9 oz. frozen lingonberries (available in some speciality food stores and online)
100 g/^{1}/$_2$ cup caster/granulated sugar

Cream gravy

meat stock
1 tablespoon plain/all-purpose flour
a good glug of single/light cream
sea salt and freshly ground black pepper, to taste

Serves 6

If using oats, soak them in the meat or chicken stock for 5 minutes.

Mix the minced/ground meat with a good pinch of salt for a couple of minutes in a food processor to ensure it's blended thoroughly.

Add the eggs, flour, spices and Worcestershire or soy sauce to another bowl and mix with the soaked oats or breadcrumbs and grated onion, then add this to the meat mixture. You'll have a sticky, but mouldable, mixture. Leave the mixture to rest for 20–25 minutes before using.

Heat up a frying pan/skillet with a small knob/pat of butter or oil and shape one small meatball. Fry it until done and then taste it. Adjust the seasoning according to taste and fry another meatball to test it until you get it just right.

Shape the individual meatballs in your hands – it helps if your hands are damp. Each meatball should be around 2.5 cm/1 inch in diameter.

Melt a knob/pat of butter in a frying pan/skillet with a dash of oil and carefully add a few meatballs – make sure there is plenty of room for you to swivel the pan round and help turn them so they get a uniform round shape and do not stick. You'll most likely need to do this in several batches. Cooking time is usually around 5 minutes per batch. Keep in a warm oven until needed.

When your meatballs are done, keep the pan on a medium heat. Ensure you have enough fat in there, if not, add a knob/pat of butter to the pan. Add a tablespoon of flour and whisk, then add a splash of stock and whisk again as you bring to the boil. Keep adding stock until you have a good creamy gravy, then add a good dollop of single/light cream and season well with salt and pepper. The colour of the gravy should be light brown.

Serve with mashed potatoes and stirred lingonberries (see page 16).

This is great bowl food to make in large batches and freeze in portions. After a quick bit of prep, you can leave this bubbling on the hob for as long as you like. It's a good one for the budget, too, with minced/ground beef, kidney beans and chopped tomatoes all very inexpensive ingredients to buy.

Chili con carne

2 tablespoons olive oil
1 red onion, finely chopped
1 garlic clove, finely chopped
800 g/1 lb. 12 oz. beef mince/
    ground beef
1 fresh chilli/chile, deseeded and
    finely chopped
a pinch of cayenne pepper,
    plus extra to serve
a pinch of ground cumin
a pinch of ground coriander
2 teaspoons dark muscovado/
    molasses sugar
1 tablespoon plain/all purpose flour
a pinch each of sea salt and freshly
    ground black pepper
1/2 beef stock/bouillon cube
    (or 30 g/1 oz. veal stock)
a 400-g/14-oz. can kidney beans,
    drained (drained weight
    250 g/9 oz.)
1 tablespoon tomato purée/paste
100 ml/1/3 cup red wine
200 g/7 oz. canned chopped
    tomatoes
rice and sour cream, to serve

Serves 4

Heat the oil in a saucepan or deep frying pan/skillet over medium heat and fry the onion and garlic for about 4–5 minutes until they just start to brown.

Add the beef mince/ground beef and fry for another minute, using a wooden spoon to break up the meat.

Add the chilli/chile, cayenne pepper, cumin, coriander, sugar, flour and some salt and pepper, and stir until it forms a paste. Then slowly crumble in the beef stock/bouillon cube or add the veal stock.

Then add the kidney beans, tomato purée/paste, red wine and chopped tomatoes and bring to the boil.

Once it bubbles, reduce the heat to low and let it simmer for 45 minutes, or up to an hour if you can, so that it thickens.

Serve straight away with rice, a dollop of sour cream and a pinch of cayenne pepper on the top.

Chilli con carne freezes brilliantly: portion it into freezerproof containers or sandwich bags and freeze for up to 3 months. Once defrosted, just check the flavours and add a little chilli/chili powder, salt or cayenne pepper to liven it up a bit if necessary.

Cook the lentils separately or use store-bought, pre-cooked lentils to make this dish easier to do on a weeknight. If you don't have a tagine, a cast-iron pot or Dutch oven work well too. But the presentation of a tagine gives a dramatic touch when entertaining!

Moroccan chicken tagine with brown lentils

2 teaspoons olive oil
1 teaspoon cumin
1 teaspoon ground coriander
a pinch of sea salt
a pinch of freshly ground
    black pepper
a drizzle of vegetable oil
2 chicken breasts, bone and skin
    kept on
1 onion, chopped
250 ml/1 cup chicken stock
6–8 dried whole Turkish apricots,
    soaked in water for 10 minutes
1 orange, peeled and cut in wedges
8 pitted green olives
2 garlic cloves, crushed
1 teaspoon cinnamon
190 g/1 cup dried green or
    brown lentils
a handful of fresh flat-leaf parsley,
    to garnish

Serves 2

First, mix the olive oil, cumin, coriander, cardamom, salt and pepper in a bowl. Then scoop the spice mixture under the chicken skin breast, as evenly as possible, coating the two breasts. Reserve any excess mixture.

In a large stove-top tagine, heat the vegetable oil on medium–high heat. Then add chicken, skin side down to brown the skin, and cook for 5 minutes. Remove the chicken and set aside. Remove any excess chicken fat but leave a little to coat the base of the tagine.

In the same tagine, add the onion with half of the chicken stock and fry for 8 minutes, or until the onion is translucent. Add the chicken, skin side up, the soaked apricots, orange wedges and olives, and the rest of the spice mixture. Turn the heat to low and cook for 40 minutes.

Rinse the dried lentils. Then put them in a separate medium saucepan or pot over high heat with the water. Bring to the boil, then reduce the heat and simmer, uncovered for 30–40 minutes, adding 480 ml/2 cups of water if required so the lentils are always just covered.

Remove the chicken from the tagine and cover in foil to keep warm. Then add the cooked lentils, the remaining 60 ml/^{1}/$_4$ cup of chicken stock and mix together with the apricots, orange wedges and olives, making sure everything is mixed together and hot.

Using a slotted spoon, plate a generous scoop of the lentil mixture and put the chicken on top. Drizzle with a little extra sauce from the pan and garnish with fresh flat-leaf parsley.

A seriously addictive and healthy salad bowl that makes a perfect dinner on a warm evening. If you don't have time to poach the chicken yourself, shred the meat from a store-bought barbecue chicken or a Peking duck from Chinatown.

Asian chicken noodle salad

400 ml/1²/₃ cups coconut milk
grated zest and freshly squeezed juice of 1 lime
700 g/1½ lbs. (about 5) chicken breasts
1 tablespoon palm sugar
500 g/18 oz. vermicelli glass noodles
100 g/1¾ cups beansprouts
30 g/generous ½ cup coriander/cilantro, chopped
30 g/generous ½ cup fresh mint, chopped
2 carrots, cut into matchsticks
1 cucumber, halved, deseeded and cut into matchsticks

4 spring onions/ scallions, finely sliced
1 long red chilli/chile deseeded and cut into thin strips
50 g/½ cup peanuts, toasted (optional)
75 g/¾ cup fried crispy shallots (optional)

Dressing

1 fresh red chilli/chile, deseeded and finely chopped
1 garlic clove, crushed
4 tablespoons fish sauce
2 tablespoons palm sugar
2 tablespoons freshly squeezed lime juice
2 teaspoons soy sauce

Serves 6

Begin by poaching the chicken. Combine the coconut milk, lime juice and zest in a saucepan or pot big enough to hold the chicken breasts in one layer. Set over medium heat, until bubbles start to appear on the surface. Add the chicken to the pan and bring to the boil. Immediately reduce the heat and gently simmer for about 10 minutes, until the chicken is just cooked.

Lift the chicken breasts out of the pan using a slotted spoon and put on a baking sheet to cool. Set the poaching liquid to one side.

To make the dressing, pound the chilli/chile and garlic to a paste in a pestle and mortar. Add the remaining ingredients, mix then set aside.

Put the noodles in a bowl and cover with boiling hot water. Set aside to soak for about 15 minutes.

When the chicken is cool, shred the meat finely and add 60 ml/¼ cup of the reserved poaching liquid to keep it moist.

Drain the noodles using a colander and put in a large serving bowl. Add the shredded chicken, beansprouts, coriander/cilantro, mint, carrot, cucumber, spring onions/scallions and chilli/chile. Pour over a little of the dressing and use your hands to mix everything together.

Top the salad with the toasted nuts and fried shallots, if desired, and serve with the remaining dressing on the side.

FRESH FISH
AND SEAFOOD

Here a brown rice base is used for a more, nutty, less refined source of carbohydrate and if you can find brown sushi rice, use that. Otherwise you can use a short grain or even regular long grain brown rice. Check packet instructions for varying cooking times.

Go green sushi bowl

150 g/³/4 cup brown sushi rice
2 tablespoons chopped fresh
 coriander/cilantro, plus a few
 leaves to serve
2 tablespoons soy sauce
2 tablespoons rice wine vinegar
1¹/2 tablespoons mirin
2 teaspoons caster/granulated sugar
1 teaspoons wasabi paste
2 tablespoons sesame seeds
1 avocado
250 g/9 oz. skinless raw salmon
 and kingfish mixed
30 g/scant 1 cup rocket/arugula
 (handful)
100 g/1 cup shredded mangetout/
 snow peas
50 g/¹/2 cup shelled edamame
 beans or shelled broad beans
50 g/2 cups seaweed salad
 (shop bought)

Serves 2

First, cook the rice. Put it in a saucepan with 300 ml/1¹/4 cups cold water and bring to the boil. Add a little salt, cover and cook over low heat for 25 minutes. Remove from the heat, but leave undisturbed for a further 10 minutes until the rice is tender. Drain if necessary and transfer to a large bowl.

Whisk together the chopped coriander/cilantro, soy sauce, vinegar, mirin, sugar and wasabi paste until smooth. Stir half into the rice and leave rice to go cold.

Just before serving prepare remaining ingredients. Toast the sesame seeds in a dry frying pan/skillet over medium heat, stirring for 2 minutes or until browned. Let cool.

Peel, stone/pit and slice the avocado. Cut the salmon and kingfish into sashimi slices about 3 mm/¹/8 inch in thickness. Trim and thinly shred the mangetout/snow peas.

Divide the cooled rice between 2 bowls and arrange all the other ingredients on top. Drizzle over the remaining dressing and serve.

Poké is a raw fish salad dish from Hawaii and you can see the influence of Japanese flavourings with seaweed and sesame seeds, a regular addition to the dish. It is often combined with melon and cucumber giving it a refreshingly different flavour. Here the quinoa base adds a truly international appeal.

Poké (tuna) bowls with melon and cucumber salad, red quinoa and crispy ginger

100 g/½ cup red quinoa
a 5-cm/2-inch piece of ginger
1 tablespoon avocado oil
1 tablespoon light soy sauce
1 tablespoon white wine vinegar
2 teaspoons caster/granulated sugar
sunflower oil, for deep-frying
1 tablespoon wakame seaweed
1 avocado
½ melon (about 350 g/¾ lb.), peeled, seeded and diced
½ cucumber, peeled, seeded and diced
2 spring onions/scallions, trimmed and thinly sliced
200 g/7 oz. fresh skinless tuna, diced
1 tablespoon black sesame seeds

Serves 2

Cook the quinoa according to packet instructions. Transfer to a bowl.

Peel the ginger and grate 1 teaspoon into a bowl. Whisk in the avocado oil, soy sauce, vinegar and sugar, stirring until the sugar is dissolved. Stir into the quinoa and leave to cool.

Thinly slice and then shred the remaining ginger. Heat a little sunflower oil in a frying pan/skillet and deep-fry the ginger for about 1 minute until crisp and golden. Drain on paper towels.

Soak the wakame seaweed in a little boiling water for 5 minutes until softened. Drain well and pat dry with paper towels.

Peel, stone/pit and dice the avocado. Add to a bowl with the melon, cucumber and spring onions/scallions. Add in the diced tuna and gently mix together.

Divide the quinoa between two bowls and arrange the other ingredients on top scattering the sesame seeds and crispy ginger over the top.

A California roll in a bowl with inspiration taken from perhaps the world's most famous and loved sushi combo. In this bowl Japanese pickled mushrooms have been included, which are delicious, but any Japanese pickles can be substituted.

California sashimi bowls with sticky rice

150 g/³/₄ cup sushi rice
1 tablespoon sushi seasoning (see Tip)
25 g/¹/₄ cup sesame seeds
1 tablespoon caster/granulated sugar
2 tablespoons soy sauce
1 tablespoon hot water
1 spring onion/scallion, finely chopped
1 carrot
¹/₂ cucumber
100 g/3¹/₂ oz. broccoli
100 g/3¹/₂ oz. crab sticks
100 g/3 cups shredded iceberg lettuce
¹/₄ sheet nori seaweed
25 g/¹/₄ cup Japanese pickled mushrooms (see Tip)

Serves 2

Put the rice in a bowl and cover with cold water, stir well, strain and then return to the bowl. Cover again with cold water and leave to soak for 30 minutes. Strain and rinse again. Put rice in a small saucepan with 175 ml/²/₃ cup of cold water. Bring to the boil, cover and simmer very gently for 20 minutes. Remove from the heat and leave undisturbed for a further 5 minutes. Transfer to a bowl, stir in the sushi seasoning and leave to cool completely.

Next, prepare the dressing. Put the sesame seeds, sugar, soy sauce, hot water and spring onion/scallion in a spice grinder or small blender and blend until as smooth as possible. Set aside.

Just before serving, trim the carrot and cut into fine julienne. Likewise with the cucumber, but no need to peel it. Cut the broccoli also into wafer thin slices (the florets will crumble, but that's fine). Cut the crab sticks into thin shreds. Cut the nori into thin strips.

Divide the lettuce between the bowls and arrange the sushi rice on top. Cover with the prepared vegetables and pickled mushrooms. Drizzle over the dressing and finish with the nori strips.

Tip: Sushi seasoning and Japanese pickles are available from Asian food stores.

Pho is a Vietnamese version of a traditional French consommé-based soup. Brill is the perfect fish for this bowl because it is a wonderfully mild-flavoured, yet firm fish, so it will hold together and enable the consommé to remain clear.

Brill pho

1 kg/35 oz. whole brill
2 carrots, peeled and chopped
1 brown onion, peeled and
   chopped
2 celery stalks/ribs, chopped
2 garlic cloves, peeled and
   thinly sliced
2 shallots, peeled and thinly sliced
20 ml/1 1/2 tablespoons sesame oil
a small bunch of fresh coriander/
   cilantro, finely chopped, leaves
   reserved to garnish
1 teaspoon fish sauce (Nam Pla)
6 spring onions/scallions,
   thinly sliced
freshly squeezed juice of 1 lime,
   plus 1 lime, cut into wedges

Serves 4

Fillet and skin the brill. Use the bones, skin, carrots, onion and celery to make a clear fish stock. Put all of the ingredients in a large pan set over low–medium heat, Cover with 1 litre/1³/₄ pints of water, bring to a low simmer and cook for 15 minutes. Reduce the heat and continue to cook for a further 45 minutes. Pour the liquid through a fine-mesh sieve/strainer into a jug/pitcher and discard the pulp.

Put the garlic and shallots with the sesame oil in a large saucepan set over low heat. Add the brill fillets and fry with just enough heat to cook but not to caramelize. Add 2 teaspoons of the chopped coriander/cilantro.

Pour the stock into the pan and bring to a gentle simmer. Add a little fish sauce to season, then add the spring onions/scallions.

Pour in the lime juice and divide the pho between serving bowls. Garnish with coriander/cilantro leaves and a wedge of lime.

Tip: A delicious variation of this recipe is to use fresh prawns/shrimp and/or scallops when they are in season. The light saltiness of the prawns/shrimp and scallop meat balances well with the delicate Vietnamese flavours and the prawn/shrimp heads and scallop frills make the most wonderful stock.

This basic Vietnamese-style soup encapsulates a real taste of spring within a bowl. Shrimp are a great source of low-fat protein whilst pea shoots are extremely easy to grow yourself both inside and out.

Shrimp, pea and pea shoot soup

350 g/12 oz. dried rice stick
   noodles
1.25 litres/2 pints chicken stock
1 small onion, sliced
4 garlic cloves, roughly chopped
2 red bird's eye chillies/chiles,
   pounded
6 kaffir lime leaves, pounded
2.5 cm/1 inch galangal, sliced
   and bruised
2 lemon grass stalks, trimmed
   and bruised
3 tablespoons fish sauce
2 tablespoons freshly squeezed
   lime juice
1 tablespoon grated palm sugar
2 celery sticks, sliced
2 tomatoes, peeled, deseeded
   and diced
500 g/7½ cups (about 50) medium
   prawns/shrimp, peeled and
   de-veined
150 g/3 cups peas
a handful of pea shoots
a handful of fresh herbs, such as
   perilla leaves and coriander/
   cilantro

Serves 4

Soak the noodles in a bowlful of hot water for 20–30 minutes until softened. Drain well, shake dry and set aside.

Put the stock, onion, garlic, chillies/chiles, lime leaves, galangal and lemon grass in a saucepan set over medium heat and bring to the boil. Simmer gently for 10 minutes until the soup is fragrant, then strain the stock through a fine-mesh sieve/strainer into a clean saucepan.

Stir in the fish sauce, lime juice and sugar, and set over medium heat. Add the celery and tomatoes and simmer for 5 minutes. Add the prawns/shrimp and peas, and simmer for a further 2–3 minutes, until the prawns/shrimp are just cooked through.

Divide the noodles between bowls and pour over the soup. Serve topped with pea shoots and herbs.

Gremolata is a zesty mixture of parsley, lemon zest and garlic, sometimes combined with olive oil, that is used in many classic Italian dishes. Here it is used to balance the richness of hot smoked salmon. The addition of buttery cannellini beans make this a delicious and satisfying salad.

Hot smoked salmon and cannellini bean salad bowl with gremolata

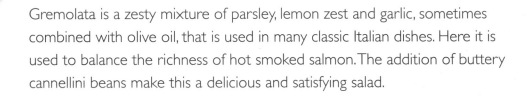

leaves from a bunch each of
   fresh flat-leaf parsley and mint,
   roughly chopped
1 garlic clove, crushed
1 teaspoon finely grated lemon
   zest
2 tablespoons freshly squeezed
   lemon juice
65 ml/¼ cup extra virgin olive oil
400 g/14 oz. hot-smoked salmon
   fillet
a 410-g/14-oz. can cannellini beans,
   drained and well rinsed
2 small red onions, thinly sliced
1 cucumber, peeled, split
   lengthways, deseeded and
   sliced into crescents
1 large handful baby spinach leaves
sea salt and freshly ground
   black pepper, to taste

Serves 4

To make the gremolata, combine the parsley, mint, garlic, lemon zest and juice and oil in a small bowl.

Roughly flake the salmon into a large bowl and add the beans, onions, cucumber and spinach leaves. Season to taste with salt and pepper and toss to combine. Serve immediately with the gremolata on the side as a spooning sauce.

Vegetarian option: Replace the salmon with 400 g/14 oz. firm smoked tofu or tempeh (an Indonesian speciality that has a nuttier, more savoury flavour than tofu), cut into thin slivers, and add a handful of roughly chopped fresh coriander/cilantro leaves for extra flavour.

Probably the best known of all Thai dishes, pad Thai in its simplest form is a basic combination of fried noodles with tofu, egg and beansprouts. Fresh cooked prawns/shrimp add a touch of luxury to the dish.

Shrimp pad Thai

250 g/9 oz. dried rice stick noodles
4 tablespoons peanut
   or vegetable oil
2 garlic cloves, sliced
24 prawns/shrimp, peeled and
   de-veined
125 g/1 cup firm tofu, diced
2 eggs, lightly beaten
4 spring onions/scallions, trimmed
   and cut into 2.5-cm/1-inch
   lengths
1 tablespoon dried shrimp
125 g/2 cups beansprouts, trimmed,
   plus extra to serve
2 tablespoons chopped fresh
   coriander/cilantro

Sauce

2 tablespoons grated palm sugar
2 tablespoons fish sauce
2 tablespoons freshly squeezed
   lime juice
1 tablespoon tamarind water
   (see Note)
2 teaspoons light soy sauce

To serve

peanuts, crushed
a pinch of cayenne pepper
1 lime, cut into wedges
coriander/cilantro leaves

Serves 4

Soak the noodles in a bowlful of hot water for 20–30 minutes until softened. Drain well, pat dry with a clean kitchen cloth and set aside in a large mixing bowl.

Whisk all the sauce ingredients together in a small mixing bowl and set aside.

Heat 2 tablespoons of the oil in a wok or large frying pan/skillet set over medium heat. Add the garlic and fry for 30 seconds, remove with a slotted spoon and set aside. Add the prawns/shrimp to the pan and stir-fry for 2 minutes until cooked, remove with a slotted spoon and set aside.

Add the tofu to the pan (with a little more oil, if needed) and stir-fry for 4–5 minutes until crispy. Pour the beaten egg into the pan and cook, stirring gently until it sets around the tofu. Remove with a slotted spoon and break up roughly.

Add the remaining oil to the pan and stir-fry the spring onions/scallions and dried shrimp for 2 minutes until the onions are softened. Stir in the noodles, prawns/shrimp, garlic, tofu mixture and the sauce, stirring constantly until everything is heated through. Stir through the beansprouts and coriander/cilantro.

Transfer the noodles to serving dishes, sprinkle over the peanuts, cayenne pepper and leaves and serve with lime wedges and extra beansprouts.

Note: To make tamarind water, dilute three parts of tamarind concentrate with two parts water.

This is not meant to be an authentic Kashmir curry by any stretch. It's a bit 1970s with the bananas included but that's what helps this curry bowl combine its mild flavour with nutty and fruity flavours. This is a truly filling bowl perfect as a midweek meal for the family.

Kashmir shrimp curry

2 brown onions, peeled and chopped
3 garlic cloves, peeled and chopped
2 x 5-cm/2½-inch pieces of fresh ginger, peeled and thinly sliced
vegetable oil, for frying
2 teaspoons Masala spice blend (see Note)
1 teaspoon ground turmeric
200 g/2 cups ground cashew nuts
400 g/2 cups canned chopped tomatoes
50 g/⅓ cup sultanas/golden raisins
300 g/1¾ cups long-grain rice
1 teaspoon nigella/black onion seeds
2 tablespoons flaked/slivered almonds
1 tablespoon fennel seeds
500 g/18 oz. uncooked peeled prawns/shrimp
1 firm banana, peeled and sliced into 5-mm/¼-inch rounds
sea salt, to taste

Serves 4

Firstly make the base for the curry using the onions, garlic and ginger – if you like curry it's worth making multiples of this base and freezing it. Put the onions, garlic and ginger in a large saucepan and just cover with water. Set over low heat and bring to a low simmer for 30 minutes. Purée the mixture after cooking with a handheld electric blender. If you can, make this the day before and leave to infuse in the fridge overnight.

Cover the base of a large frying pan/skillet with a thin coating of oil and set over medium heat. Once hot, add the masala spice blend and turmeric, then once the spices start to release their aroma, add the ground cashew nuts. Heat for a couple of minutes then add the base mixture, chopped tomatoes and sultanas/golden raisins and bring to a gentle simmer.

In another saucepan add 600 ml/2 cups of water and a pinch of salt and bring to a simmer over medium heat. Add the rice, bring back to a simmer then take off the heat, cover and leave for 15 minutes, when the rice will be cooked.

Heat a little oil in a small saucepan set over medium heat and add the almonds, nigella and fennel seeds. Warm until they pop and the almonds colour to a light golden brown. Remove from the heat and set aside.

Add prawns/shrimp to the sauce and simmer for 5 minutes then add the banana. Stir in carefully and after another 5 minutes, the curry should be ready to serve. Taste the sauce and add a little salt to season.

Serve with the cooked rice and dress with a sprinkle of the toasted almonds, fennel and nigella seeds to add some flavour explosions and texture to the finished dish.

Note: To make a Masala spice blend at home, preheat a frying pan/skillet over medium heat. Put 1 teaspoon each of whole cloves and cumin seeds, 1 tablespoon of coriander seeds, 3 black peppercorns, ½ teaspoon of ground turmeric and ½ star anise in the dry pan and swirl until strongly aromatic. Take off the heat and grind to a powder with a pestle in a mortar.

This subtle Cambodian curry remains largely unknown to western audiences. It is usually thickened with eggs and steamed in banana leaves, but here it is cooked on the stove without the eggs. However, if you would prefer it cooked in a more traditional way there is a note below with instructions how to do so.

Monkfish amok curry

vegetable oil, for frying
4 shallots, thinly sliced
a 400-ml/14-fl. oz. can coconut milk,
  plus extra to serve
2 tablespoons coconut palm sugar
5 teaspoons fish sauce
150 g/1 heaping cup green beans
400 g/14 oz. monkfish, cut into
  bite-size pieces
1 fresh red chilli/chile, thinly sliced
2 kaffir lime leaves, very thinly
  sliced
boiled or steamed jasmine rice,
  to serve

Amok curry paste

2 fresh red chillies/chiles, deseeded
5 garlic cloves, peeled
2 stalks lemongrass, trimmed,
  outer leaves removed
5 shallots or 1 red onion
5 kaffir lime leaves
3-cm/1 1/4-inch piece of galangal,
  peeled, or 2-cm/3/4-inch piece
  of fresh ginger
1 teaspoon ground turmeric
grated zest of 1 lime

Serves 4

For the amok curry paste, add everything to a food processor with 3 tablespoons of water and blitz until you have a paste, scraping down the sides when needed. This will take at least a few minutes of constant blitzing.

Put a large pot with 2 tablespoons of vegetable oil over medium heat. Add in the shallots and stir-fry for a few minutes until softened. Turn down the heat, add in the curry paste and cook gently for 5–10 minutes until fragrant. Add in the coconut milk, 200 ml/3/4 cup of water, sugar and fish sauce. Bring to a boil, reduce the heat to low and simmer for 3 minutes. Add in the green beans and fish and cook for a further 5–8 minutes until the fish is just cooked through and beans are tender. Ladle into a bowl and spoon a little coconut milk on top. Scatter over the sliced chillies/chiles and kaffir lime leaves and serve the rice on the side. If you like you can line the bowl with a banana leaf to serve. To do this, fold in the edges of the banana leaf and secure with a cocktail stick/toothpick.

Traditional method: Preheat the oven to 180°C (360°F) Gas 4. Omit the green beans. After you have simmered the coconut milk, sugar and fish sauce for 5 minutes, remove and leave until almost cool. Add in 2 eggs and mix well to combine.

Add in the fish pieces. Line a small ovenproof dish with a banana leaf and pour in the curry. Sit the dish on a baking sheet and put in the oven. Pour boiling water into the sheet surrounding the dish to create a bain-marie. Cook in the oven for 15 minutes. The curry should be a slightly set-custard consistency. Scatter over the sliced red chilli/chile and lime leaves and serve with rice.

Jícama is a great vegetable on its own and, as here, in coleslaw. Walk into your local sushi chain and it's easy to see that sesame seeds are often used for presentation. But they actually give a nutritional punch of calcium and magnesium to this bowl as well!

Sesame seared tuna with Asian slaw

40 g/¹/₃ cup mixed black and
   white sesame seeds
2 × 170-g/6-oz sushi grade tuna
   pieces
2 tablespoons grapeseed oil
sea salt and freshly ground
   black pepper, to taste

Asian slaw

250 g/1 cup sliced jícama
¹/₂ mango, sliced in long strips
100 g/2 packed cups thinly sliced
   red cabbage

Tamari sauce

1 tablespoon soy sauce
   (check for gluten-free)
2 teaspoons sesame oil
¹/₄ teaspoon finely sliced ginger
2 teaspoons flaxseed oil
2 teaspoons clear honey
1 tablespoon freshly squeezed
   lemon juice
1 tablespoon white sesame seeds
a handful of fresh coriander/
   cilantro, to garnish

Serves 4

Spread the black and white sesame seeds evenly on a plate. Season each side of tuna with salt and pepper. Then coat each side of the tuna with the seed mixture – don't forget the sides as well. In a grill pan, heat the grapeseed oil over medium–high heat. Once the oil is hot, sear the tuna for 30 seconds on all 4 sides. Remove from the pan and set aside.

For the Asian slaw, cut the jícama, mango and cabbage into long strips.

Whisk all the ingredients for the tamari sauce together in a bowl. Add the slaw and mix it all together.

To serve, thinly slice the tuna steak. Spoon a generous amount of slaw on each plate and put the sliced tuna on top. Garnish with fresh coriander/cilantro.

So many cured meats come from warm Southern European plains where there's a sea breeze and sunshine on the roofs… However, this is a stew recipe that's perfect for when it's chilly outside and you need some central heating for the tummy. The chorizo and chilli/chile provide the most amazing warmth.

Scallop, chorizo and quinoa stew with herb dumplings

20 g/generous 1 tablespoon butter
1 red onion, diced
1 garlic clove, chopped
1 red (bell) pepper, deseeded and diced
2 celery stalks/ribs, chopped
100 g/3¾ oz. chorizo, diced
1 small fresh red chilli/chile, deseeded and finely chopped
1 teaspoon paprika
30 g/scant ⅓ cup plain/all-purpose flour
500 ml/generous 2 cups chicken stock
100 g/3¾ oz. quinoa or pearl barley
200 g/7 oz. shelled scallops
sea salt and freshly ground black pepper, to taste

Herby dumplings (optional)

50 g/⅓ cup shredded suet
100 g/¾ cup self-raising/rising flour
a pinch of dried thyme
a pinch of dried rosemary
a baking sheet, greased

Serves 2

For the stew, melt the butter in a frying pan/skillet, then fry the onion and garlic over low heat for 10 minutes, until softened. Add the red (bell) pepper and celery, and fry until the vegetables soften. Add the chorizo, red chilli/chile and paprika, and season with salt and pepper, then stir to mix. Sprinkle the flour over the top and stir for just a minute before adding the chicken stock. Stir in the quinoa.

Bring to a simmer and simmer for 35 minutes, stirring occasionally, then add the scallops. Cook for a further 10 minutes (or 15 minutes if the scallops are frozen), until the scallops are cooked.

If you would like to make the herby dumplings, start making them as soon as the stew begins simmering.

Preheat the oven to 180°C (350°F) Gas 4.

Put all the dumpling ingredients in a bowl and stir to mix, then gradually add 50–100 ml/scant ¼–⅓ cup of cold water, a little at a time, and keep mixing with your hands until the mixture comes together in a solid ball. Don't make the mixture too wet, otherwise the dumplings will be soggy.

Divide and roll the mixture into round dumplings and put them onto the prepared baking sheet. Bake in the preheated oven for 15 minutes, then add them to the stew for the last 25 minutes of cooking time. Serve hot.

Index

A

açaí bowls galore 20
adzuki beans: healing adzuki bean stew 44
sesame-coated tofu with adzuki beans 51
alfalfa sprouts: kimchi, avocado and alfalfa salad 75
artichoke salad with spelt grains 39
Asian chicken noodle salad 117
aubergine (eggplant):
smoked aubergine and red pepper salad 88
avocados: kimchi, avocado and alfalfa salad 75

B

bananas: matcha tea, banana and sesame smoothie bowl 12
beef: chili con carne 113
Korean-style mapo tofu 93
lemongrass beef in betel leaves 106
real Swedish meatballs 110
Vietnamese-style beef salad 97
beetroot (beet): warm ham hock, beetroot and lentil salad 101
berry chia compote 23
bibimbap 109
black beans: black bean bowl with chimichurri dressing 52
Cuban black bean and red pepper soup 36
sweet potato noodles with broccoli in black bean sauce 76
breakfast bowls: chia seed breakfast bowl 19
omega-3-rich breakfast bowl 27
brill pho 126
broad beans (fava):
slow-cooked lamb salad with 98
broccoli: sweet potato noodles with broccoli in black bean sauce 76

C

California sashimi bowls 125
cannellini beans: hot smoked salmon and cannellini bean salad bowl 130
cauliflower: cauliflower soup 64
oven-roasted Romanesco cauliflower, labne and spiced nuts 72
cheese: heirloom tomato and griddled feta on orzo 68
mozzarella cheese, chilli and green bean bowls 84
chia seeds: berry chia compote 23
chia seed breakfast bowl 19
chicken: Asian chicken noodle salad 117
chicken soup with black forbidden rice 102
Moroccan chicken tagine 114
spirulina green chicken salad 94
chillies: chili con carne 113
mozzarella cheese, chilli and green bean bowls 84
chorizo: scallop, chorizo and quinoa stew 141
claypot, mushroom 87
coconut yogurt with berry chia swirl 23
compote, berry chia 23
crab: California sashimi bowls 125
Cuban black bean and red pepper soup 36
cucumber: poké bowls with melon and cucumber salad 122

curry: Kashmir shrimp curry 134
monkfish amok curry 137
raw curry with jícama rice 83

D F

dimsum duck wonton soup 105
dumplings, herb 141
falafel, pea and mint 48
fennel: pink quinoa salad with fennel and arame 47
feta: heirloom tomato and griddled feta on orzo 68
fish see salmon; tuna, etc

G H

granola: honey and vanilla granola bowl 31
savoury granola 40
green beans: mozzarella cheese, chilli and green bean bowls 84
gremolata 130
ham: warm ham hock, beetroot and lentil salad 101
healing adzuki bean stew 44
healing miso soup 67
heirloom tomato and griddled feta on orzo 68
hemp tabbouleh 48
horchata smoothie, Mexican 15

J K

jícama rice, raw curry with 83
kale: spaghetti squash with tofu, nori and kale pesto 55
Kashmir shrimp curry 134
kimchi, avocado and alfalfa salad 75
kingfish: go green sushi bowl 121
Korean-style mapo tofu 93
koshari bowl 56

L

labne, oven-roasted Romanesco cauliflower and 72
lamb salad, slow-cooked 98
lemongrass beef in betel leaves 106
lemons: lemon tahini sauce 48
preserved lemon dressing 68
lentils: brown lentil and Swiss chard soup 35
koshari bowl 56
Moroccan chicken tagine 114
warm ham hock, beetroot and lentil salad 101
lingonberries, stirred 16, 110

M

mackerel: spiralized summer salad 71
mapo tofu, Korean-style 93
matcha tea, banana and sesame smoothie bowl 12
meatballs, real Swedish 110
melon and cucumber salad 122
Mexican horchata smoothie 15
mint: pea and mint falafel 48
miso: healing miso soup 67
miso dressing 79
monkfish amok curry 137
Moroccan chicken tagine 114
Moroccan pumpkin stew 43
mushrooms: mushroom claypot 87
teriyaki tofu with shiitake mushrooms 80

N

noodles: Asian chicken noodle salad 117
noodle salad 106
shrimp pad Thai 133
soba noodles with miso

dressing 79
sweet potato noodles
with broccoli in black
bean sauce 76
teriyaki tofu with shiitake
mushrooms and soba
noodles 80
nori: spaghetti squash with
tofu, nori and kale pesto
55

O P
oat and rye porridge with
lingonberries 16
omega-3-rich breakfast
bowl 27
orzo, heirloom tomato and
griddled feta on 68
pad Thai, shrimp 133
pea shoots: shrimp, pea and
pea shoot soup 129
peas: pea and mint falafel 48
shrimp, pea and pea shoot
soup 129
peppers: Cuban black bean
and red pepper soup 36
smoked aubergine and
red pepper salad 88
pesto, spaghetti squash with
tofu, nori and kale 55
pho, brill 126
poké bowls with melon and
cucumber salad 122
polenta: soft polenta with
yogurt and sesame seeds
32
pomegranate, slow-cooked
lamb salad with 98
pork: bibimbap 109
real Swedish meatballs 110
yota 59
porridge: oat and rye
porridge 16
rye-bread porridge with
skyr 24
pumpkin stew, Moroccan 43

Q R
quinoa: pink quinoa salad 47
poké bowls with melon

and cucumber salad and
red quinoa 122
scallop, chorizo and
quinoa stew 141
rice: bibimbap 109
California sashimi bowls
with sticky rice 125
chicken soup with black
forbidden rice 102
go green sushi bowl 121
Kashmir shrimp curry 134
koshari bowl 56
raw curry with jícama rice
83
rye-bread porridge 24
rye flakes: oat and rye
porridge 16

S
salads: artichoke salad with
spelt 39
Asian chicken noodle
salad 117
Asian slaw 138
heirloom tomato and
griddled feta on orzo 68
hot smoked salmon and
cannellini bean salad
bowl 130
kimchi, avocado and alfalfa
salad 75
melon and cucumber
salad 122
mixed leaves with savoury
granola 40
mozzarella cheese, chilli
and green bean bowls 84
noodle salad 106
pink quinoa salad 47
slow-cooked lamb salad
98
smoked aubergine and
red pepper salad 88
spiralized summer salad
71
spirulina green chicken
salad 94
Vietnamese-style beef
salad 97
warm ham hock, beetroot

and lentil salad 101
salmon: go green sushi bowl
121
hot smoked salmon and
cannellini bean salad
bowl 130
sashimi bowls, California 125
scallop, chorizo and quinoa
stew 141
sesame seeds: matcha tea,
banana and sesame
smoothie bowl 12
sesame-coated tofu with
adzuki beans 51
sesame seared tuna with
Asian slaw 138
soft polenta with yogurt
and sesame seeds 32
shrimp: Kashmir shrimp
curry 134
shrimp pad Thai 133
shrimp, pea and pea shoot
soup 129
skyr, rye-bread porridge
with 24
smoothie bowls: matcha tea,
banana and sesame 12
Mexican horchata 15
soups: brill pho 126
brown lentil and Swiss
chard soup 35
cauliflower soup 64
chicken soup 102
Cuban black bean and red
pepper soup 36
dimsum duck wonton
soup 105
healing miso soup 67
shrimp, pea and pea shoot
soup 129
super spring greens soup
63
spelt, artichoke salad with
39
spiralized summer salad 71
spirulina green chicken
salad 94
spring green soup, super 63
squash: spaghetti squash
with tofu, nori and kale

pesto 55
stews: healing adzuki bean
stew 44
koshari bowl 56
Moroccan pumpkin stew 43
scallop, chorizo and
quinoa stew 141
yota 59
super spring greens soup 63
sushi bowl, go green 121
Swedish meatballs, real 110
sweet potato noodles with
broccoli in black bean
sauce 76
Swiss chard: brown lentil
and Swiss chard soup 35

T
tabbouleh, hemp 48
tagine, Moroccan chicken 114
tofu: healing miso soup 67
Korean-style mapo tofu
93
sesame-coated tofu with
adzuki beans 51
spaghetti squash with
tofu, nori and kale pesto
55
teriyaki tofu with shiitake
mushrooms and soba
noodles 80
tomatoes: heirloom tomato
and griddled feta on orzo
68
tuna: poké bowls with
melon and cucumber
salad 122
sesame seared tuna with
Asian slaw 138

V W Y
Vietnamese-style beef salad
97
wontons: dimsum duck
wonton soup 105
yogurt: coconut yogurt with
berry chia swirl 23
soft polenta with yogurt
and sesame seeds 32
yota 59

Recipe Credits

Brontë Aurell
Artichoke salad with spelt grains
Oat and rye porridge with lingonberries
Real Swedish meatballs
Rye-bread porridge with skyr and toasted hazelnuts

Miranda Ballard
Chili con carne
Scallop, chorizo, chilli and quinoa stew with herby dumplings

Ghillie Basan
Smoked aubergine/eggplant and red pepper salad

Jordan Bourke
Bibimbap
Korean-style mapo tofu
Monkfish amok curry
Teriyaki tofu with shitake mushrooms and soba noodles

Ross Dobson
Brown lentil and Swiss chard soup
Hot smoked salmon and cannellini bean salad with gremolata
Slow-cooked lamb salad with broad/fava beans, pomegranate and fresh mint

Mat Follas
Brill pho
Kashmir shrimp curry

Amy Ruth Finegold
Cauliflower soup with roasted pumpkin seeds
Chicken soup with black forbidden rice
Moroccan chicken tagine with brown lentils

Sesame seared tuna with Asian slaw

Nicola Graimes
Black bean bowl with chimichurri dressing
Kimchi, avocado and alfalfa salad
Mixed leaves with savoury granola
Mozzarella, chilli/chile and green bean salad
Sesame-coated tofu with adzuki beans
Soba noodles with miso dressing
Vietnamese-style beef salad
Warm ham hock, beetroot/beet and lentil salad

Dunja Gulin
Chia seed breakfast bowl
Healing adzuki bean stew with amaranth
Healing miso soup
Koshari bowl
Mushroom claypot
Omega-3 rich breakfast bowl
Pink quinoa salad with fennel and arame
Soft polenta with yogurt and sesame seeds
Yota

Vicky Jones
Black-eyed beans and squash in coconut milk
Cuban black bean and red pepper soup

Uyen Luu
Lemongrass beef in betel leaves

Louise Pickford
California sashimi bowls with sticky rice
Dimsum duck wonton soup
Go green sushi bowl

Heirloom tomato and griddled feta on orzo with lemon dressing
Matcha tea, banana and sesame smoothie bowl
Mexican horchata smoothie bowl
Oven-roasted Romanesco cauliflower, labne and spiced nuts
Poké (tuna) bowls with melon and cucumber salad, red quinoa and crispy ginger with a light ginger dressing
Shrimp pad Thai
Shrimp, pea and pea shoot soup
Sweet potato noodles with broccoli in black bean sauce

Shelagh Ryan
Asian chicken noodle salad

Janet Sawyer
Honey and vanilla granola bowl
Spiralized summer salad with smoked mackerel

Sarah Wilkinson
Moroccan pumpkin stew
Spaghetti squash with tofu, nori and kale pesto
Super spring greens soup

Jenna Zoe
Açaí bowls galore
Coconut yogurt with berry chia swirl
Hemp tabbouleh with pea and mint falafel
Raw curry with jícama rice

Caroline Artiss
Spirulina green chicken salad

Photography Credits

Jan Baldwin
Page 75

Martin Brigdale
Page 94

Peter Cassidy
Pages 17, 24–25, 34, 38, 61, 98, 99, 111, 131

Tara Fisher
Pages 81, 82, 136

Erin Kunkel
Page 118

Adrian Lawrence
Pages 42, 56, 85

David Munns
Page 35

Steve Painter
Pages 4–6, 30, 54, 55, 112, 127, 135, 140

William Reavell
Pages 2-3, 10–11, 16, 18, 23, 28, 37, 44–47, 65, 73, 74, 79, 84, 87, 101, 121

Matt Russell
Pages 41, 48–49, 60, 64, 68, 77, 86, 92-93, 96, 97, 100, 114

Toby Scott
Pages 26, 29, 33, 50, 53, 78

Ian Wallace
Pages 9, 12–15, 27, 67, 89-91, 104, 105, 119, 120, 123–125, 128–129, 132–133

Kate Whitaker
Pages 1, 8, 31, 39, 57, 108, 109, 116, 117, 138

Clare Winfield
Pages 19, 21, 22, 32, 58, 59, 62, 63, 69, 71, 72, 76, 83, 95, 102, 103, 107, 113, 115, 126, 130, 139